SERIES E...

Colin MacCabe and David Meeker
SERIES CONSULTANTS

Cinema is a fragile medium. Many of the great classic films of the past now exist, if at all, in damaged or incomplete prints. Concerned about the deterioration in the physical state of our film heritage, the National Film and Television Archive, a Division of the British Film Institute, has compiled a list of 360 key films in the history of the cinema. The long-term goal of the Archive is to build a collection of perfect show-prints of these films, which will then be screened regularly at the Museum of the Moving Image in London in a year-round repertory.

BFI Film Classics is a series of books commissioned to stand alongside these titles. Authors, including film critics and scholars, film-makers, novelists, historians and those distinguished in the arts, have been invited to write on a film of their choice, drawn from the Archive's list. Each volume presents the author's own insights into the chosen film, together with a brief production history and a detailed filmography, notes and bibliography. The numerous illustrations have been specially made from the Archive's own prints.

With new titles published each year, the BFI Film Classics series will rapidly grow into an authoritative and highly readable guide to the great films of world cinema.

Could scarcely be improved upon ... informative, intelligent, jargon-free companions.
The Observer

Cannily but elegantly packaged BFI Classics will make for a neat addition to the most discerning shelves
New Statesman & Society

How did they ever
make a movie of
LOLITA ?

METRO-GOLDWYN-MAYER presents in association with SEVEN ARTS PRODUCTIONS JAMES B. HARRIS and STANLEY KUBRICK'S LOLITA

Starring JAMES MASON · SHELLEY WINTERS · PETER SELLERS as "Quilty" and Introducing SUE LYON as "Lolita"

Directed by STANLEY KUBRICK · Screenplay by VLADIMIR NABOKOV based on his novel "Lolita" Produced by JAMES B. HARRIS

APPROVED BY THE PRODUCTION CODE ADMINISTRATION

BFI FILM

CLASSICS

LOLITA

. . . .

Richard Corliss

BRITISH FILM INSTITUTE

bfi

BFI PUBLISHING

First published in 1994 by the
BRITISH FILM INSTITUTE
21 Stephen Street, London WIP IPL

The British Film Institute exists
to encourage the development of film, television
and video in the United Kingdom,
and to promote knowledge, understanding and
enjoyment of the culture of the moving image.
Its activities include the National Film and Television
Archive; the National Film Theatre;
the Museum of the Moving Image;
the London Film Festival; the production and
distribution of film and video; funding and support for
regional activities; Library and Information Services;
Stills, Posters and Designs; Research,
Publishing and Education; and the monthly
Sight and Sound magazine.

British Library Cataloguing-in-Publication Data.
A catalogue record for this book is available from the
British Library.

ISBN 0-85170-368-2

Designed by
Andrew Barron & Collis Clements Associates

Typesetting by
Fakenham Photosetting Limited, Fakenham, Norfolk

Printed in Great Britain by
The Trinity Press, Worcester

CONTENTS

. . . .

ACKNOWLEDGMENTS

· ·

For information and insights on Nabokov, Kubrick and the making of *Lolita*, I thank Alfred Appel, Jr., James B. Harris, Nikki Smith and David Thomson. For many kindnesses, appreciation goes to Jytte Jensen, David Lerner, David Meeker and Markku Salmi. For insights and indulgence, I am grateful to my friends at *Time* magazine, especially Elliot Ravetz and Carrie Ross Welch. For patience and care, thanks to editor Ed Buscombe. And, for life, to Mary Corliss: light and fire, sin and soul.

The picture of Nabokov on p. 8 is courtesy of Penguin Books.

PALE FILM

....

I was the shadow of the monarch seen
Through the false window of the movie screen.
I was the fine phrase buried in a film style:
A simile debased into a smile.
I was the words that pictures rarely talk of
In movies made from novels by Nabokov.
I was Vladimir's book van, made to stall
Because it ran into a Kubrick wall.

I was the nymphet Hum could not possess
10   Because she'd grown into a Lioness
And lost her schoolgirl power to enchant –
A Tuesday Weld pursued by Cary Grant.
I was the movie usherette whose spark
Lit furtive, fatal laughter in the dark;
I was the vermin Hermann, who would snare
A twin – stunt double for his mad despair;
I was the man who filled his nuptial void
With robot paramours: King, Queen, And Droid.
Enfin, I was the novelist who watched
20   As each of his books-into-films was botched.

I'm speaking to you now through the façade
Of that imperious impaler, Vlad,
Not of the real Nabokov, who'd admit
That film was more to me, and I to it.
I intersected with the movies' gaze
As Humbert saw the young Dolores Haze:
A lissome, coarse, naive, beguiling witch,
A moving picture framed in gilded kitsch,
A kitten in American fake fur
30   To warm a European connoisseur.

Thus Hollywood to me: a pasture full
Of pretty creatures, barnyard words, and bull.
I used to like to visit theatres where

I'd see a comedy by René Clair,
A Marxist stateroom scene, a Hardy laugh,
The languor of a starlet's downy calf.
But I preferred the sweat behind the sweet,
The chewing gum beneath the velvet seat;
The couple coupling in the back row, blind
40   To their huge doubles on the screen entwined;
The picture fans whose fondest hopes were clipped
From the posh lustre of a Metro script.
To them, the dearest dream ethereal;
To me, the merest raw material.
I took these film-besotted wretches and
Applied to them my writer's sleight-of-hand:
Albinus K., producer, movie-lorn;
Lolita H., recruit for Quilty's porn;
Herr Hermann K., sad cinemaniac . . .

50   But never V. Nabokov, movie hack.
Oh, once I was a picture writer in
The would-be Russia of Weimar Berlin.
And more than once my slim form was allowed
To peer out of a movie-extra crowd:
The larval author lurking in costume,
As Hitchcock did, or Vivian Darkbloom.
A few years later, I was nearly flown
To Hollywood to work with Milestone.
But when my camera shuttered, I withdrew
60   To see what my true muse would lead me to.

A generation passed. A nymphet kissed
The ear lobe of an aging novelist.
Then, from the pulpit, censors read the bans
And damned my 'dirty book' without a glans.
They made the child famous, made me rich
And raised again my movie-writing itch.
When Kubrick put my darling on the screen,
I saw my words made whispers, twelve made teen,
Back roads made backlots, US made UK.

70 And green made gold, and me an émigré
From Lo, whom I conceived but could not save.

Except for that grand gaffe, I never gave
The pictures in my head to film. I could
Be paid, but not betrayed, by Hollywood.
Fitzgerald might have fallen there – a fawn
Caught in the klieg lights of a mogul's yawn –
But not I. I could gauge the camera's lure
And still know how to shade the aperture.

So let film versions of my novels reek
80 Of grimy hands upon some choice antique.
I know those nitrate reels will decompose.
But each good reader will preserve my prose,
And his creative memory will save
My *Laughter in the Dark* and *King Queen Knave*.
He'll play the true *Lolita* and *Despair*
In his cinémathèque imaginaire.

Here lies Nabokov: teacher, critics' pet,
Daft lepidopterist (nut with a net),
A portraitist of haunted souls, who paints,
90 In pastel, lurid eyes: a beast's, a saint's,
A monster humanised when he's unmanned.
And here flies V. N.'s work through movieland:
A butterfly in the projector beam.
It floats, then flits away, as in a dream
Of monarchs who find freedom in a cage
With horizontal bars – lines on a page.
To readers, not to viewers, falls the task
Of tiptoeing into the cage to ask:
Who was that monarch? What did he mean?

COMMENTARY

....

Line 1 (a): I was the shadow

'Lolita, light of my life, fire of my loins. My sin, my soul.'

Of the four great novelists of this century (Proust, Joyce, Nabokov, Fulmerford), Vladimir Nabokov is the only one whose muse summered in cinema. Among world-class directors, Stanley Kubrick the one most closely associated with film adaptations of novels.

Nabokov called *Lolita* 'my best work in English', and that judgment seems modest today. Kubrick called his film of *Lolita* his one manifest failure. 'Had I realised how severe the [censorship] limitations were going to be,' he told *Newsweek* in 1972, 'I probably wouldn't have made the film.' In 1987, he admitted to *Der Spiegel* that the limitations went beyond those of censorship to his timidity in translating a novel whose glory was in its unique narrative voice. 'If it had been written by a lesser author,' Kubrick said, 'it might have been a better film.'

They might both be right, and there still would be a reason for this little book. A novel, even the novel Nabokov completed in 1954, may have aspects that can be expressed more delicately or pertly on screen. A film, even the film Kubrick and his producing partner, James B. Harris, made in 1961–2, may mark only one stage, and not necessarily the highest, in the continuing life of a work of fiction. Each may reveal the boundaries of the other, if only by crossing them or tiptoeing around them. In the thirty-two years since *Lolita*'s release, the ghosts of novel and film still hunt and haunt each other – as if they were Humbert Humbert, world-renowned paedophile, and Clare Quilty, his evil twin in their mirrored pursuit of young Dolores Haze, alias Lolita.

Nabokov's cross and joy was knowing that he wrote for himself and posterity. He risked his bijou reputation and his university position for a book about 'a man who liked little girls'. His early fears that the novel might never be published in America were, for four agonising years, justified. Yet he did not compromise *Lolita*'s story or style. The work cost him nothing but agony.

Kubrick's joy and cross was that of any artist addressing a touchy topic in a mass medium in 1962: to know that everyone could see his work, but that the work would be a compromise between the artist's ambitions and his patron's apprehensions. The film cost its backers

$1,750,000, a tenth of the price tag for the same year's *Mutiny on the Bounty* but nonetheless real money. Hollywood-style movies were still part of a mass medium. Each picture was expected to appeal, potentially, to everyone and, more important, to offend no one. Megamillion-dollar 'art movies' – not the kind of weird filth that Quilty made (*see note to line 48*), but the kind that *Lolita* might have been, heedless of studio hindrance or popular head-scratching, in some ideal parallel universe – were a few years away, and Kubrick would sire the breed with *2001: A Space Odyssey* (1968). The rambunctious depiction of teen sexuality would follow a few years after that: *A Clockwork Orange* (1971). Then the exhaustively judicious adaptation of a difficult novel: *Barry Lyndon* (1975). And then the exposé of a haunted writer abusing a precocious child: *The Shining* (1980).

It happens that Nabokov wrote *Lolita* at exactly the right moment for its artistic and commercial success. Within a few years of his completing it, the Supreme Court in the US and Parliament in the UK had liberalised statutes protecting the written word.

It happens that Kubrick directed *Lolita* at just the wrong moment. Within a few years of his completing it, American film-makers would take their cue from Europeans and force an 'adult' cinema on their sponsors and their audience. Nabokov could write an 'unprintable' novel, then bide his time for a more tolerant judiciary and less timid publishers. But Kubrick could not, really, make an 'unreleaseable' picture; outrage was not an option. We must consider, then, not the film that this gifted director might have made, but the one that he did.

This was a May–September romance. The writer and the director collided at the apogee of Nabokov's genius and the early flowering of Kubrick's film mastery. The day *Lolita* opened, Nabokov was 63 and had been writing fiction for nearly forty years; Kubrick, 33, had been directing features for fewer than ten. If one were to chart Kubrick's career, *Lolita* would represent a promise and a frustration. If one were to chart Nabokov's, the novel could be seen on the highest plateau, nestled among three other surpassing works he wrote between the late 1940s and 1961: *Conclusive Evidence* (his autobiography, revised later as *Speak, Memory*), *Pnin* (his novel about a Russian who teaches at an American college), and *Pale Fire* (another brilliant evocation of genius and insanity). And on this elevated plain would be the peak of *Lolita*.

An analysis of any other Kubrick adaptation, from *The Killing* to

Full Metal Jacket, would place the author of the novel in a supporting role to the author of the film. *Lolita*, though, is different: a glowing masterpiece made into an appealing apprentice-piece. So in this study, Nabokov will receive at least as much attention as Kubrick. He has earned it, just as Humbert's dark majesty overwhelms Dolly Haze's coltish allure. For in a way Nabokov *was* Humbert, an educated, widely experienced European come to America; and Kubrick was Lolita, a creature still in the process of becoming. Only his pupa, the film, was left behind, frozen in time.

Line 1 (b): the monarch

Nabokov was born, in 1899, into spectacular wealth. In his second score of years he was reduced, like so many of his countrymen, to impoverished émigré status in Berlin and Paris. The climax of Nabokov's next twenty-year exile – in the United States, where he pursued his passion for lepidoptery, collecting butterflies in the American West, and his profession of teaching literature at Wellesley College and Cornell University – came with the 1958 US publication of *Lolita*, which brought the author a plusher version of the wealth and station that was his as a youth. Finally, in the sunset quarter of his life, Nabokov was pleased to play the snooty lord of a Swiss palace, indulging his double-domed prejudices with Alpine hauteur.

The author enjoyed dismissing most films as rubbish, and claimed no special interest in the medium. He cheerfully told Alfred Appel, Jr., author of *Nabokov's Dark Cinema*, that he did not see *Citizen Kane* until 1972 (though, when he did, he declared it 'Extraordinary! A masterpiece!'). Nor did star quality make much impression on him. At a Hollywood party in 1960, Nabokov asked one tall, rugged gent what he did for a living. 'I'm in pictures,' John Wayne replied.

Nabokov was in pictures too. He appeared in them; he wrote them; he wrote about them. The success of *Lolita* ensured that his oeuvre would become a lending library to movies. *Laughter in the Dark*, *Despair* and *King, Queen, Knave*, in various dwarf mutations, became theatrical films in the 60s and 70s. And in telling ways, films enticed Nabokov. As raw material they influenced his writing and the elegant strategies to which he submitted them. The typical Nabokov novel is a palace of trick mirrors and trap-doors that lure the reader into a more vivid and terrifying 'reality' (one of the few words which mean nothing without quotes) His books' typical protagonist is a sad psychopath, captive in a private darkroom, where cinematic nightmares spin out of his head and into his life. Hermann Karlovich, the murderer in *Despair*, and Albinus and Margot, the dupe and super duper of *Laughter in the Dark*, are not just mad. They are movie-mad.

Line 2: window of the movie screen

Lolita is the confession, the jailbird narrative, of Humbert Humbert, a European scholar who has come to teach in America. Spending the summer as a lodger in the New England home of the widow Charlotte Haze, he falls in lust with Charlotte's young daughter Dolores, nicknamed Lolita. Humbert marries Charlotte to be close to the object of his obsession. Charlotte discovers Humbert's diary, in which he has recorded his 'nympholepsy', and, blinded by insight, she dies in a freak accident (rain, car). Humbert takes Lolita, who does not immediately know of her mother's death, away from the summer camp she had been attending and on a long drive to his teaching post at Beardsley College; on this trip, at the Enchanted Hunters Hotel, she initiates the sexual affair he has dreamed of. At Beardsley the natural abrasion of any two people learning to live together is intensified by Humbert's jealousy and the girl's restlessness. After a row the two leave Beardsley for a cross-country trip, during which Humbert becomes convinced that they are being followed. He is right. Clare Quilty, a playwright who had idly seduced Charlotte, is tracking them and having sex with the girl in her few free moments. Lolita leaves Humbert for Quilty, from whom she soon flees. Four years later, married and pregnant, she writes to Humbert asking for money. He gives it to her, learns Quilty's identity and, realising that he loves this bloated teenager who long ago shed her nymphic allure, begs Lolita to leave with him. She refuses. Humbert discovers Quilty's address, finds him at home, and kills him. The murderer dies in prison after completing this book, his confession.

The Nabokov novel was seen through several windows; Kubrick's movie screen was only the most prominent. Here are a few stages of the butterfly's metamorphosis:

The novel. Nabokov began the book in 1947 and completed it in the spring of 1954. It was published by the Olympia Press in Paris in 1955, by G. P. Putnam's Sons in the United States in 1958, and by Weidenfeld and Nicolson in Britain in 1959.

The album. In 1959, Nabokov read excerpts from *Lolita* for a spoken-word record issued by Caedmon.

The screenplay. Nabokov wrote a script for Kubrick in the summer of 1960. In the fall, Kubrick and Harris abridged and rewrote the script. Peter Sellers, who played Clare Quilty in the film, introduced additional dialogue into his role.

The film. Kubrick shot the movie at Associated British Studios (Elstree) for eighty-eight days in 1961. The film, starring James Mason as Humbert, Sue Lyon as Lolita and Shelley Winters as Charlotte, had its world premiere on 13 June 1962, at Loews State Theatre in New York City.

The published screenplay. Nabokov rewrote his *Lolita* script and published it, as *Lolita: A Screenplay*, in 1974.

The musical. In 1971 the Broadway-style musical *Lolita, My Love* opened in Philadelphia, closed for renovations, reopened for five days. To ho-Hummable music by John Barry (*Born Free*), Alan Jay Lerner's lyrics felicitously restored Lolita's nymphetry ('A demi-Delilah ... a guileless beguiler') and Humbert's seraphic perversion ('Dante exploded/ As Petrarch and Poe did./ And this is the story/ In all its nymphic glory/ That I shall dwell on'). In the fashion of Henry Higgins (*My Fair Lady*), Gaston Lachaille (*Gigi*) and King Arthur (*Camelot*), Lerner's Humbert was an aloof gentleman with an unusual taste in young women. Lerner wanted Richard Burton for the role, but John Neville starred as Humbert. Dorothy Loudon played Charlotte and Leonard Frey was Quilty. The show, like Humbert, was taken ill on the road while the nymphet escaped; *Lolita, My Love* closed in Philadelphia and died there.

The play. In 1981 a stage adaptation, written and directed by Edward Albee, played briefly on Broadway. In 1962, a clever mogul might have thought that the movie version of *Lolita*, where a man and his child lover argued over the pretence that she was a grown woman, should be written by the author of *Who's Afraid of Virginia Woolf?*, where a grown-up couple argued over the pretence that they had a child. But the *Lolita* that Albee did finally write had no lyric spirit, no faithful wit. Shirley Stoler, the concentration camp ogress in Lina Wertmuller's *Seven Beauties*, played Charlotte, and lost. Other conspirators were Donald Sutherland (a dyspeptic Humbert), Clive Revill (a puckish Quilty, wanting menace), Blanche Baker (Carroll Baker's daughter; a senescent Lo). Ian Richardson, declaiming excerpts from the novel, was the evening's *raisonneur*.

The remake? In 1990 Carolco, the muscular independent film outfit (*Rambo*, *The Terminator*), paid $1 million to secure the remake rights for director Adrian Lyne. He and *Lolita* seemed a match made in New Hollywood heaven. Lyne had made a drama of precocious girls facing life's ordinary outrages (*Foxes*), a young woman's coming-of-age musical (*Flashdance*), a steamy tale about a sadomasochistic liaison (*9½ Weeks*), a popular thriller with a sexual kink (*Fatal Attraction*), and a deathbed memoir streaked with nightmare paranoia (*Jacob's Ladder*). Since then, Lyne has filmed *Indecent Proposal*, in which a young woman chooses to have sex with an older man for her own good reasons: to use him and help the fellow she really loves. But Carolco suffered financial reverses after buying the property, and Lyne has yet to present a script to Dmitri Nabokov, the novelist's son, who has consultation rights.

Line 6: movies made from novels by Nabokov

Life is a goddess, says a character in Nabokov's 1927 short story 'The Passenger', 'whose works are untranslatable, indescribable. ... All that's left to us is to treat her creations as a film producer does a famous novel, altering it beyond recognition ... for the sole purpose of having an entertaining film unfold without a hitch ... with an unexpected but all-resolving outcome.'

    Kubrick and Harris solicited Nabokov for the film rights to *Lolita* in the summer of 1958, a few weeks before the American publication date. The two men had made *The Killing* and *Paths of Glory* – cheap but handsome calling cards to present to a famous author. It's also possible that Nabokov was impressed by their association with the novelist Calder Willingham (*End as a Man*), who had helped write the *Paths of Glory* script and whose 'magnificent talent' Nabokov had praised in a March 1958 letter. For $150,000, plus 15 per cent of the producers' profits, he handed *Lolita* into their care. They asked if Mr Nabokov would also care to write the screenplay. He would not.

A year later Willingham had written an adaptation of *Lolita* and Kubrick had rejected it. Again the director telegraphed Nabokov: 'Book a masterpiece and should be followed even if Legion and Code disapprove.' The Legion of Decency was the Roman Catholic film ratings group that exerted powerful pressure on Hollywood film-making; the Production Code was the censorship arm of the movie companies. In 1956 the Legion had condemned Elia Kazan's *Baby Doll* (also about a middle-aged man whose child bride is stolen away by a wilier rival), and in 1955 the Production Code withheld approval from Otto Preminger's *The Man With the Golden Arm*, a film about heroin

James B. Harris with Sue Lyon

addiction. But no major-studio picture had yet flouted condemnation from both groups.

This time Nabokov agreed to write the script, though he later said he knew that 'infinite fidelity may be an author's ideal but can prove a producer's ruin. . . . All I could do in the present case was to grant words primacy over action, thus limiting as much as possible the intrusion of management and cast.' So the old Russian threw himself, with his usual informed energy, into reimagining his story for movies.

Movies, of course, are the director's game; the director of *Lolita* knew that, and so, we warrant, did the screenwriter. For tactical reasons Kubrick decided to be courteous to the celebrated novelist. But he would not be cowed by him. Or by the received opinion that *Lolita*, in style and content, would prove impervious to adaptation. 'If it can be written or thought,' Kubrick said, 'it can be filmed.'

We think he meant: 'If I can think it, I can film it.' But would Nabokov be able to transfer his thoughts about *Lolita* into script form? The author thought so: 'The screenplay became poetry,' he said in 1962, 'which was my original purpose.' Harris and Kubrick ostensibly agreed; they told Nabokov the script was 'the best screenplay ever written in Hollywood'. Yet according to Harris in 1993, Nabokov's huge script was unfilmable. 'You couldn't make it. You couldn't *lift* it.'

Line 8 (a): Kubrick

Nabokov's father was a Russian statesman of the liberal stripe whose anti-Soviet politics and love of learning informed the life of young Vladimir Vladimirovich. (In Berlin exile in 1923, the elder Nabokov would be shot dead by a tsarist assassin.) Kubrick's father was a Bronx physician who gave Stanley a camera when the boy was 13. Both the writer and the director chose their callings early; both played chess for a living, Nabokov as a teacher in Berlin, Kubrick as a 'chess hustler' at the open-air tables in New York's Washington Square; both were absolutists in their approach to art.

Kubrick was 'class photographer' at Taft High School but did not get into college. Instead, he became a staff photographer for *Look* magazine. His ambition was evident from youth; determined to make films, he made his own at twenty-one. RKO released *Day of the Flight* (1950) and *Flying Padre* (1951), the two documentary shorts he wrote, produced, directed, photographed and edited; both films displayed the aerial obsession that would soar in *2001: A Space Odyssey*.

His film of *Lolita* begins, as the novel ends, with a murder. The movie-makers had a few reasons for putting last things first, but one of Kubrick's may have been to get in the mood. Each of his previous five features were about men who kill. The first one, *Fear and Desire* (1953), about a stricken quartet of warriors, is shot in a self-consciously poetic style that Kubrick later kept in check.

Not in *Killer's Kiss* (1955), though, which mixes elements from *On the Waterfront* (a boxer who spends time on a tenement roof, lavishes attention on pets, and cares for a thin blonde girl) with the grimy trappings of mid-50s exploitation movies (seedy milieu, fist fights, a woman who removes her sweater to reveal a large black bra, a predator who mauls the girl into a submissive kiss). But Kubrick shoots it like an art-house documentary, with moody *film noir* lighting. The movie is like an existential novel with a tough-guy paperback title slapped on it for commercial purposes. The story is nothing, atmosphere is all; there is more voice-over than dialogue. The pocked faces, the empty, littered streets, the camera tricks (dramatic foregrounding, negative images) make *Killer's Kiss* seem a forgotten godfather to *Mean Streets*.

The next film, *The Killing* (1956), was Kubrick's first film with Harris, a young man of means who would also produce *Paths of Glory* and *Lolita*, and it kicked them both into the big B-movie time. The plot of Lionel White's source novel *Clean Break* was simple: seven men connive to rob a racetrack safe. But White ran his story through a slipstream of flashbacks and sideswipes, and this *Citizen Kane* of heist movies made it play smartly on screen. The success of such microscopic heist films as *The Asphalt Jungle* and *Rififi* – where the spectacle of men planning a dangerous crime was as eye-catching as a knife fight – taught Kubrick that briskness was enough. The actors needn't emote. The private lives could be instructively drab, especially those of mousy George Peatty (Elisha Cook, Jr.), a track teller, and his wife Sherry (Marie Windsor). He pampers and whines, she lounges and castrates, and Kubrick observes each whip lash with exquisite patience; the sourness runs on for minutes, often without a cut. In visual and emotional content the scenes are fine sketches for the second half of *Lolita*, when Humbert and Lo will bitch till dawn.

Kubrick moved upmarket with the Kirk Douglas war movies

Paths of Glory (1957) and *Spartacus* (1960). The first film, in which good men lose a bad battle and must pay for their officers' stupidity, might be a sequel to the second, in which good men prepare for a noble battle that cannot be won. (And both films were the director's basic training for his 1987 *Full Metal Jacket*.) *Paths of Glory* transcends the usual anti-war film clichés by giving both the grunts and the brass a misanthropic grandeur. The doomed enlisted men get the classier lighting, though: in their death cell, single-source light streams in as from a Hollywood version of Golgotha at 3 p.m.

On *Spartacus*, Kubrick was a replacement for Anthony Mann, and he rued his second-class ticket on the big train. On his debut in the grand Hollywood forum, he performed dutifully, filling the wide frame with thousands of soldiers and heaping dishes of cheesecake (Jean Simmons in her hydraulic tunic) and beefcake (Woody Strode in a jockstrap). Though the script would root for Spartacus's slaves, the movie is on Rome's side. The tone is patrician, languidly decadent – an all-night feast for Lucullan tastes.

Spartacus taught Kubrick an important lesson: temperamentally and artistically, he was unsuited to be a hired hand. *One Eyed Jacks*, the 1961 western, on which he prepared Calder Willingham's script for production only to be fired by Marlon Brando before shooting began, taught the director that there could be only one star on a Kubrick movie.

Line 8 (b): Kubrick wall

If you were to select a director to guide *Lolita* to movieland, you might want an independent spirit with a penchant for adapting novels; who is comfortable with an off-screen narrative voice; whose protagonists are sociopaths seen from the inside, neurotics outmatched by a more insidious madness; whose work addresses the corruptive power of men and the perfidy of women; who sees how abuse by someone in authority drives a young person crazy; who can locate a comedy of manners in the bleak tragedy; whose camera could glide through domestic travails, or sit still like a patient voyeur and just watch.

You would choose Stanley Kubrick. In forty years Kubrick has made twelve films, of which *Lolita* was the sixth. The first two pictures were utterly independent productions. The others were released by major Hollywood studios, but Kubrick has been an independent contractor on all but one (*Spartacus*). Whatever compromises attended the making of *Lolita* were his to consider and concede. They were not imposed on him by Seven Arts, the company that financed the film, or by Metro-Goldwyn-Mayer, the studio that released it.

Except for *Fear and Desire* and *Killer's Kiss*, which were shot from original scripts by the director's Taft High School chum Howard Sackler (later author of *The Great White Hope*), every Kubrick movie has been adapted from a novel or short story. Kubrick was the sole screenwriter of *A Clockwork Orange* and *Barry Lyndon*; Dalton Trumbo wrote the *Spartacus* script. And in those films in which Kubrick shared screenplay credit his collaborators have all been novelists: Jim Thompson on *The Killing* and *Paths of Glory*, Willingham on *Paths of Glory*, Peter George and Terry Southern on *Dr Strangelove or: How I Learned to Stop Worrying and Love the Bomb* (1964), Arthur C. Clarke on *2001*, Diane Johnson on *The Shining*, Gustav Hasford and Michael Herr on *Full Metal Jacket* (1987). And Nabokov on *Lolita*.

Each of Kubrick's films is 'narrated' in some conventional fashion by an omniscient offscreen voice (*Fear and Desire*, *The Killing*, *Paths of Glory*, *Spartacus*, *Dr Strangelove*, *Barry Lyndon*), by the protagonist (Danny in *Killer's Kiss*, Alex in *A Clockwork Orange*, Private Joker in *Full Metal Jacket*), or with title cards that set the time or place (*2001*, *Barry Lyndon*, *The Shining*). All three devices are used in the *Lolita* film.

'I've got a peculiar weakness for criminals and artists,' Kubrick said in 1957. 'Neither takes life as it is.' He presents his anti-heroes without apology or explanation: the heistmeister in *The Killing*, the generals in *Paths of Glory*, the senators in *Spartacus*, the statesmen in *Dr Strangelove*, the neurotic computer in *2001*, Alex and his Droogs, Barry Lyndon, Jack Torrance in *The Shining*, the ground-down grunts in *Full Metal Jacket*. Not to mention Humbert, madman-poet, biter bit. All these men are malignantly entertaining because they are so good at being bad; like Jack Torrance at the apogee of his madness, they shine. Each of them is offered an opportunity – money, victory, title, a job in a hotel – only to lose it. And each man will take much less pleasure in his good fortune than grief in his comeuppance. Humbert is never the triumphant Don Juan, but he is often the miserable dupe.

Evil twins abound in Kubrick films, as they do in Nabokov novels. Just when you think you've seen the worst creep in the world, a

Stanley Kubrick with Sue Lyon

more imposing maniac shows up. General Jack D. Ripper's plan to provoke a nuclear catastrophe may be insane, but Dr Strangelove's plan for life after World War III is an expression of pre-emptive evil. Brutal Alex is no match for the scientists who brain-train him. Jack Torrance may beat his child, but the Overlook Hotel whips him. *Full Metal Jacket*'s Sergeant Hartman creates a killer in Private Pyle; he should have known that the weapon would go off in his own face. And so might Humbert have known that a more expert game master would win Lolita's nickel-plated jukebox heart.

Power, education, authority corrupt – and, in Kubrick films, make a man devilishly attractive. The snakes have all the lines; it is the film-maker's way of showing their corrosive power. They use rhetoric as a weapon to deflate, deflect, distract, destroy an opponent. Their tone may be hyperbolic, like Sergeant Hartman's in *Full Metal Jacket* ('God has a hard-on for marines, because we kill everything we see'), or just plain nuts, like Ripper's in *Dr Strangelove* ('Women sense my power, and they seek the life essence. I do not avoid women, Mandrake, but I do deny them my essence'). These men without women often speak of war, and even of patriotism, in sexual terms. In *Spartacus*, the bisexual senator Crassus gives this advice to his new slave: 'There's only one way to deal with Rome, Antoninus. You must serve her. You must abase yourself before her. You must grovel at her feet. You must love her.' Crassus is, of course, 'her'. He might also be Humbert, enumerating his precepts for the conquest and adoration of Lolita.

Kubrick's is a man's world, a metaphorical boot camp. Men in authority (often of high military or political rank, sometimes just fathers or stepfathers) play with ordinary folks, and kill them for their sport. In a Kubrick film, corporal punishment is the norm. And some of it is meted out by young women, like Sherry Peatty in *The Killing*. What does *Full Metal Jacket*'s Joker read in the eyes of the Vietnamese sniper girl? I kill your friends; yet you daren't kill me. What does Kubrick's Lolita tell Humbert? You love me, I break your heart.

More often, though, a young person, male or female, suffers at the master's hands. Under this psychological torture, the victim can go mad: Ferraud (Timothy Carey) in *Paths of Glory*, Alex, Lord Bullington (Leon Vitali) in *Barry Lyndon*, Danny (Danny Lloyd) in *The Shining*. Kubrick's films are haunted by the death or disgrace of these tender cubs. In *Lolita* he saves a young girl's life – she died in the book – but deprives her of the poetic immortality Nabokov lent her.

Most Kubrick films are pitch-black comedies of manners. They can seem slow only to those viewers who aren't looking for the play of a subversive smile or an even more insolent blankness on someone's face. The comic atmosphere is often claustrophobic, but Kubrick gives his favourite actors lots of air. Timothy Carey can do his hipster routine in *The Killing*, his human-too-human whiner in *Paths of Glory*. A glummer performer can become a kind of living sculpture for Kubrick's camera. The main difference between Sterling Hayden's heist executive in *The Killing* and his nut-case general in *Dr Strangelove* is the difference between a camera at medium-range eye level and a camera that crouches at Hayden's feet and stares up his flaring nostrils.

As a voracious moviegoer in New York, young Kubrick came to admire the cascading camera movement in the films of Max Ophuls. Kubrick's movie subjects were ruder, burlier than Ophuls'; his frequent theme was man marching to an Armageddon within himself, not woman gliding to the waltz of love and death. But Kubrick films are full of long tracking shots: in the trenches, redoubts and barracks of *Paths of Glory*, *Barry Lyndon* and *Full Metal Jacket*, and in *The Shining*'s hotel corridors and maze. *Spartacus* has many long master-shots that allow the viewer a peek into naughty high life from a hiding place just a bit too far away. Look but don't touch. The movie screen may look like a window, but it is really a Kubrick wall.

Line 9: the nymphet

'Now I wish to introduce the following idea,' Humbert writes, 'Between the age limits of nine and fourteen there occur maidens who, to certain bewitched travellers, twice or many times older than they, reveal their true nature which is not human, but nymphic (that is, demoniac); and these chosen creatures I propose to designate as "nymphets".'

The poetic expression of a grotesque notion – how very Humbert! Nymphets (girls who appeal to a man's exotic tastes) 'reveal' themselves to 'bewitched travellers'; the children, then, are Circe sirens, the men mere music lovers swayed by their song. By this logic, any man who feels a drumbeat in his priapic pulse when he sees an attractive woman is absolved of the consequences. The little witch made me do it, Your Honour: the defendant's claim in a rape case. In his farewell note before leading the Los Angeles police on a low-speed chase, O. J. Simpson declared himself an 'abused spouse'.

And yet ... Humbert *is* the nymphets' love slave, and he doesn't touch them. He exploits their nearness by caressing them only in his mind; the brush fire in his trousers never spreads to their pleated skirts. He corrupts them secondhand, from behind the opaque mirror of his gallant cunning. Lolita, remember, seduces Humbert, the poor trembling, lovesick swain. He's crazy about everything she is, has and does; she can cross her legs, chew gum, shrug, mess up her room, and a lightning spasm shivers through him. He loves her arrogance towards Charlotte. He has a lover's myopia: he thinks Lolita is unique, the nymphet of all nymphets. He will later discover that she is only a kid, with a kid's convulsive whims and fleeting attention span. She can slip out of his crush when she develops one of her own, on Quilty.

Humbert is an artist, with an artist's eye for texture and style. For him, the subject for a perfect work of art is also the object of a nympholept's fantasies. It is the appeal (sexual or aesthetic) of the potential, the budding, the almost ready. It's the attraction of a mind and body struggling against cellular decay for a mind and body that can only become brighter, fuller, *more*. It's the desire to possess a child on the cusp of womanly self-consciousness, to mould that malleable flesh, that larval sensibility, like a sculptor-teacher.

The clinical name for the child lover's ailment is pederosis (a disease in which 'eros' lurks). Humbert, as well as Nabokov, hopes that the indulgent reader will see the poignancy in this condition. Humbert is in love not with people so much as with a time: a few years on the cusp of pubescence, when certain girls wander into Oz, and black-and-white becomes a rainbow. But nympholepsy is like falling in love with a piece of fruit: the object ripens and withers with the season. So Humbert kept wandering, bewitched, in search of other little deadly demons – until he met a girl who stirred in him a passion that would not ebb when she ceased to be a nymphet.

Here is the book's crucial sentence: 'I had fallen in love with Lolita forever; but I also knew she would not be forever Lolita.'

Line 10 (a): because she'd grown

Cinema used to believe in Eden. In silent movies, youth was a state of innocence, an unsullied nap in the womb. Seen today, the earliest films also have the sheen of innocence – or its scruffier fraternal twin, naiveté.

When in film history did Lolita's siblings first appear? When did children become sex objects? The obvious answer is: in retrospect. The roguish wink of hindsight can turn Mary Pickford, who was twenty-seven when she played the twelve-year-old Pollyanna, into a radical deconstructor of her own screen text. The Gish sisters can seem like white sisters due to be ravaged by their Humbert, D. W. Griffith.

Silent film abstracted images, stories and stars; soft-focus lighting aestheticised and sanctified every face. It also made actors look younger. Sound film did just the reverse. Now the camera aged its stars, and the microphone demanded the crackling sass of people who had seen it all and wanted to talk about it. Studio bosses cast Jean Harlow as a silky slut, and Loretta Young an everyday-gorgeous working girl or wife, before they were eighteen. Joan Leslie was a radiant fifteen (Sue Lyon's age during the *Lolita* shoot) when she played Gary Cooper's sweetheart in *Sergeant York*, sixteen when she was Mrs James Cagney in *Yankee Doodle Dandy*; both men were around forty.

Sexuality was for the adult actors. In this period, the moppets didn't have It. Universal and MGM encased their nymphet-aged stars, Deanna Durbin and Judy Garland, in romantic vehicles, but they were always girls in school pageants on a spectacular scale. Margaret O'Brien was no nymphet; she was merely a prodigiously torrid actress, pumping up every dinner-table dilemma into tearful tragedy. To find sensual precocity you had to look in the corners of movies – in a vagrant early moment of *The Dark Angel* (1935), for example, where seven-year-old Cora Sue Collins warms herself at a fireplace by lifting her nightgown, fore and aft, to the heat! To discover sexual intensity you had to go to Bonita Granville's performances, on the brink of teenhood, as the tattling schoolgirl in *These Three* (where her febrile jealousy makes her a sister to Charlotte Haze), and as the leader of the would-be witch pack in *Maid of Salem* (where her sexual hysteria prefigures some of Lolita's screeching scenes with Humbert).

Then there was Shirley Temple. Today she seems a wind-up doll, a showbiz distillation of kid stuff, but to Graham Greene in the 30s, Temple was the nymphic goods. Reviewing *Captain January* ('a little depraved, with an appeal interestingly decadent'), Greene wrote that Temple had 'a coquetry quite as mature as Colbert's and an oddly precocious body as voluptuous in grey flannel trousers as Dietrich's'. His 1937 piece on *Wee Willie Winkie* in *Night and Day* magazine provoked a law suit from the child's movie studio because he had puckishly suggested that Temple was an adult midget in kid's garb. To atone for what the Court called 'this gross outrage', the defendants agreed to pay £3,500 to Temple and Fox. Years later, in 1955, Greene offered crucial encouragement to another writer accused of misusing a child in print (*see note to line 63*).

Line 10 (b): Lyoness

The summer of '55 is when it all changed. For the first time a rock-'n'-roll record, 'Rock Around the Clock' by Bill Haley and the Comets, hit the top of the US charts. *Blackboard Jungle*, which used the Haley song as its anthem, made juvenile delinquency fashionable, in some circles mandatory. And from the atomic mushroom cloud that hovered like a dark brainstorm over most horror movies a powerful new species was hatched: teens. They were no longer kids and they were not yet adults, nor did they want to be; in the Kingdom of Teen, parents were the occupying army. Teens had their own language, mores, attitude galore and disposable income. They loved noise, leather and cashmere, jitterbugging, drag racing, gobs of hair grease – accoutrements to the joy and threat of sex. And what big sister had, kid sister wanted. Teen age didn't begin at thirteen; it could start at nine, like nymphetry. That summer in America, childhood officially ended.

Hollywood's cult Queen of Teen in the 50s was Tuesday Weld. At fourteen, in Leo McCarey's *Rally Round the Flag, Boys!* (1957), she played a prototypical sex kitten with the pre-James Bond babe name of Comfort Goodpasture. If the film of *Lolita* had been made in 1955, the year it was published, Weld would have been almost too perfect for the title role. Her elegant lips curled into a grin that said, 'This is where we start.' It was an invitation to schoolyard debauchery.

The mouth of the decade, though, belonged to Elvis: baby-doll lips poised between pout and sneer; Bardot's adults-only mouth, but on a man. It was a billboard advertising sex. How appropriate, then, that those lubricious, Presleyan lips should ornament the face of Sue Lyon, the movie Lolita. She was fourteen when she was cast, fifteen when she completed the film. If she seemed an older sister to Nabokov's Lolita,

Lyon did bear a resemblance, as Kubrick told biographer Alexander Walker, to Annabel Leigh (*see note to line 26*), who in the novel is young Humbert's first love: 'honey-coloured skin', 'thin arms', 'brown bobbed hair', 'long lashes', 'big bright mouth'. Whether the girl incarnated Annabel or Lolita, Nabokov approved of the choice. 'No doubt about it,' he said, 'she is the one.'

The film-makers had good reasons to cast Lyon. She proved to be a splendid young actress here, because she had the gift of 'behaving' and not 'acting'. Though this was her first starring role, she appears impervious to the strain and challenge of *Lolita*'s notoriety. She fits into the film's tempo, never rushing or pressing. So often she appears to be humouring Humbert by deigning to talk to him; like many a child for whom all adult chatter is static, she rarely accords him her full attention. She is at first a coquette, then at times bored, and occasionally she leaps into a tantrum. But she never shows fear, the kind of intuitive apprehension a child might feel at the sight of an approaching man with lust in his smile. Lyon's Lolita is interested in Humbert the way a tigress is interested in a gazelle: as pretty prey. And once she knows she has Hum's undivided obsession, she tunes out and pursues a more elusive male. It is a wonderful portrait of the banality of lust.

Sue Lyon in *Lolita*

Some scenes the actors can bring alive by the force of their technique; in some their craft colludes with their screen personality; in others the scene creates the performance. Here's a minute of *Lolita* where all three apply, but none would work without Lyon's slow sizzle. Humbert is in the rear of the shot, facing us, suggesting to Lo that they share the hotel room bed on which she is lying prone, her slim legs sticking up in the foreground, the high heels on her feet waving languidly. While they bandy, Lolita pushes off the pump on her left foot with the toe of the pump on her right foot, and then the second shoe with the stockinged toe of her left foot. The gesture would be casual, unconscious, if the girl were alone, but it has an erotic tension because a man who wants to go to bed with her is a few inches away. Hum's eyes flick up briefly at the spectacle; he is encouraged. Then she yawns and tells him to go to the hotel desk and ask for a cot to sleep on. She is tired; she is a little bored; she is ready, in one tantalising sense or another, for bed. And she is in charge.

In a 1962 interview, Lyon said of Lo, 'I feel sorry for her. She's neurotic and pathetic and she is only interested in herself.' Yet as an actress she never editorialises (as Shelley Winters sometimes does), never lets you see her disapproval of the character. She shows

imagination and authority in all Lolita's gestations: temptress, dominatrix and brat. Lyon fails only in suggesting, at the end, that the girl, like Humbert, is a victim of misapplied passion. But then, in this *Lolita*, she is meant to be nothing like that. Humbert is the injured party; Lo is one of the conspirators in his misery.

Line 11: enchant

Nabokov was forty, in Paris in 1939, when he wrote 'The Enchanter', a remorseless case history that represented 'the first little throb of *Lolita*'. It is the story of a Parisian, forty, with a secret itch for young girls. He cosies up to the ailing mother of an entrancing 12-year-old, hoping 'to meld the wave of fatherhood with the wave of sexual love'. When the woman dies he takes the girl on a trip to introduce her to his obsession. As she sleeps in their hotel room on their first night together, he stares at her, 'passing his magic wand above her body'. In the release after 'the sweetness came to a boil between his woolly tufts and her hip', he notices that she is 'fully awake and looking wild-eyed at his rearing nudity'. He rushes into a speeding car's headlights and, in 'this instantaneous cinema of dismemberment', he imagines 'zigzag gymnastics of lightning, spectogram of a thunderbolt's split seconds – and the film of life had burst.'

    The man in the story (no names, please) is as naively cunning as Humbert but lacking Humbert's florid wit. The invalid wife is a sullen, Simenon figure, so devoted to her grey pain that she does not trouble to mask it in pleasantries; her death is a relief to her and the reader. The child is no Lolita, aware of the spell she casts over a lonely paedophile; she is a police composite sketch, a rag doll in the gutter.

Line 12: Cary Grant

James Mason was Cary Grant in a broody mood; in *North by Northwest*, the two natty Englishmen snarl becomingly at each other like a man debating with his dark mirror image. Suave and drawling, with that haunted Heathcliff look, Mason could have posed for the self-portrait Humbert provides in the novel: 'a great big handsome hunk of movieland manhood . . . lanky big-boned woolly chested Hum Hum, with thick black eyebrows and a queer accent, and a cesspoolful of rotting monsters behind his slow boyish smile . . . Moreover, I am said to resemble some crooner or actor chap on whom Lo has a crush.' A playwright chap, actually, though Mason resembles Peter Sellers no more than Dirk Bogarde looks like Klaus Löwitsch (*see note to line 16*).

Mason had been the first choice to play Hum, according to Harris, but he was determined to do a play on Broadway. Then the film-makers approached Olivier; he said yes, but his agency (whose clients included Kubrick and Harris), dissuaded him. They asked David Niven; Niven said yes, but his agency talked him out of it. Evidently the cinematocracy was suspicious of these two kids who wanted to film *Lolita*. 'They knew,' recalls Harris, 'that we weren't going to make *Tammy*.' In the end, Mason agreed to be Humbert.

In preparing *Lolita* for film, Kubrick altered Humbert's character more subtly, and more radically, than Lolita's. His age was the same, but his rage was muted. Rather than a tale of a monster who learns too late what love is, the film-makers wanted a love story, though bitter and unfulfilled, all the way through. So Humbert could be no monster or child abuser. 'We wanted him to be the only innocent person in the piece,' Harris says. Lolita is treacherous, Charlotte is ravenous, Quilty is villainous. Humbert is just us – every person who loved below his station and above his emotional means.

Which makes Mason a strange choice for the role. He was not the Us, the extraordinary ordinary Joe, played by American star actors. Mason's screen persona was that of the Other. He was almost a male Garbo. His sepulchral beauty often hovered like an ancient curse over him and those women attracted to him. If he played the domestic brute (in *The Man in Grey*, *The Seventh Veil*, *Caught*, *The Reckless Moment*, *A Star is Born*), he absorbed as much pain as he dished out to his female partner or protégée. It was her fault, really, for thinking she could reverse the downspin of his fate. And if a Mason character tried to outsmart, overthrow or simply elude those in political power (in *Odd Man Out*, *The Desert Fox*, *5 Fingers*, *Julius Caesar*), he was doomed to failure not heroic but tragic – for he contained in himself the sins of his enemies. Fate sent him on a nonstop cruise to nowhere, in a sailboat (*Pandora and the Flying Dutchman*) or a submarine (*20,000 Leagues Under the Sea*).

But beneath the matter of his roles was the manner of his performing: the good manners of breeding, understatement, sufferance. And the famous voice: the plummy diction that could make the most

Studio portrait of James Mason

egregious proposition seem like a royal summons. These were the qualities Kubrick wanted in his screen Humbert. 'I don't recollect Stanley ever giving James any direction whatever,' said Oswald Morris, *Lolita*'s cinematographer, to Bob Baker and Markku Salmi in 1990 (*Film Dope* 45). 'Sue Lyon he directed very carefully, but James had got it all worked out already.' Both men knew that Mason had Humbert's soul in his piercing, hooded eyes. They could express agony at a glance.

Watch Mason 'behave', as a mother wants her children to (without noticing the rebellion in their well-bred voices). With Charlotte, Mason's Humbert seems to be nursing a toothache, but she never sees. When he first spies Lo, a close-up shows Mason suddenly looking ten years older; the girl's vitality makes him an instant old man. When ardent Charlotte locks him in a cha-cha embrace, he chugs along as if he were being forced to have sex but is too much the gentleman to say no. His underplaying throughout is a heroic act of discretion.

The moviegoer was his one confidant. Alone in the Haze home after Lo has hugged him goodbye on her way to summer camp, Humbert throws himself on her bed and daintily dries his eyes on her pillowcase – the professor revealing himself as a woozy teenager. Mason could also alert the viewer to *Lolita*'s occasional swatches of pre-*Strangelove* black comedy. After Charlotte's death he lounges in the bathtub, blotto to his good fortune, on his chest a cocktail tumbler that protrudes above the bathwater like a lighthouse in polluted seas, while neighbours offer their condolences and absolutions. Even Nabokov, no special admirer of the movie, saluted 'that rapturous swig of Scotch in the bathtub'; it 'struck me as appropriate and delightful.'

Humbert's maleficence explodes once only, in Mason's great, reckless moment: when he reads Charlotte's scrawled proposal of marriage. The irony in Mason's reading is homicidal. He begins with the dark and obvious tone of, say, a Cambridge undergraduate (Mason took a first in architecture there) declaiming a naive and anonymous love letter for the avid entertainment of his friends. The voice shades into foul joy with the realisation that the Haze woman has offered him an irresistible compromise: if Humbert allows Charlotte to love him and paw him, in a coarse parody of the intensity he feels for Lolita, then she will let Mr Humbert 'be a father to my little girl.' By the end, Mason's chortle is galactic in its appreciation of misery and melodrama. His Humbert might be God, Satan and mankind, black-holed into one bath-robed bachelor. He controls Charlotte's destiny, he has access to his dearest damnation, and he is ready to take the toxic bait. The scene fades out, but still we hear Mason's laughter in the dark.

Line 14: laughter in the dark

Humbert is lost in Lolita's brilliance. Albinus Kretschmar, the protagonist of *Laughter in the Dark* (the 1931 novel originally called *Camera Obscura*), is blinded by the movie light. One day he goes to a movie theatre and is dazzled by the glitter of a pert usherette, Margot. She is barely Lolita's senior – eighteen in the Russian original, sixteen in Nabokov's own English translation – and she entrances Albinus with 'the childish lines of her body'. For Margot, Albinus will desert his trusting wife Elisabeth and bankroll a fruitless film project. Albinus' Quilty-like nemesis is the cartoonist Axel Rex, one of the vilest demons in Nabokov's bestiary. In all Nabokov stories love is blind; here the myopic Albinus is literally blinded, allowing Margot and Axel to caper lewdly around him. The antecedents are obvious: Albinus = Humbert, Margot = Lolita, Elisabeth = Charlotte, Axel = Quilty.

The 1969 movie adaptation, written by playwright Edward Bond

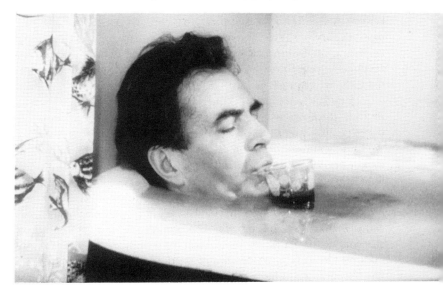

'That rapturous swig of Scotch in the bathtub'

(*Saved*) and directed by Tony Richardson (*Mademoiselle*), proved that sadism doesn't play as well as it reads. Nor is Swinging London a plausible stand-in for 1930s Berlin. To look at the picture today is to see Mod turned to mould. Anna Karina was too old for Margot, and too ready to place the nymph's childish guile into adulterous quotation marks. Jean-Claude Drouot, as Axel, capered like a satyr at a rural pageant; Satan doesn't wear quite his smirk. Only Nicol Williamson, as Albinus, approached the cruel depths of Nabokov's vision.

Line 16: despair

Cinematic doppelgängers abound in Nabokov's *Despair* published in 1934. Hermann Karlovich, a Berlin chocolate maker burdened with a lazy wife and a mind too restless to remain caged in sanity, stumbles upon his exact double, a bum named Felix, and hatches the perfect murder plot. He will dress Felix up as himself, kill the impostor, and make a clean getaway to a new life, taking his wife Lydia with him. The only problem is that Felix looks nothing like Hermann, as the police quickly discover. Poor Hermann: he is an artist – wily, imaginative, given to shapely ruses – in everything but vision. He can't see that Lydia is capable of finding anyone else attractive. And he is precisely the wrong person to devise a 'double' suicide scheme. Hermann has made an error the dullest moviegoer could see through.

   In 1978, Rainer Werner Fassbinder and Tom Stoppard made a film, and a botch, of *Despair*. Fassbinder lingers on the rasping, grasping gasping of Andrea Ferreol (Lydia), as if the story were fodder for a chic denunciation of the bourgeoisie. Klaus Löwitsch, who played Felix, is no stunt double for Dirk Bogarde, who played Hermann – and whose exquisite eyes, two brown pools of liberal anguish, suited him more for Humbert. The movie is as nasty as Hermann's intentions, but lacks the lyric pulse that beats in every Nabokov murderer.

Line 18: King, Queen

King, Queen, Knave, written in 1928, is the tale of a bored woman who takes her husband's young nephew as a lover, schemes to kill the older man, and dies before she can bring it off. *Cf.* James M. Cain, Fritz Lang, and a host of *film noiristes* whom Nabokov preceeded in this novel.

Dreyer is a wealthy Berlin clothier with a wife, Martha, slightly above his station and a young nephew, Franz, ripe for corruption by them both. While Martha exercises her hatred of Dreyer in a dalliance with Franz, Dreyer spends his evenings consulting with an inventor who has created three automatons: two men and a woman, naturally. Or as natural as anything is in the novel's clockwork world. Nabokov treats these crawly creatures with a fascinated contempt; lepidoptery, we are reminded, is a division of entomology. Dreyer, a genial philanderer and a born victim, is the least despicable of the lot. But his interest in menswear and mannequins, in status and humanoids, so envelops him that he doesn't notice his cuckoldry any more than Hermann or Albinus do. Three Nabokov men; three blind mice.

Jerzy Skolimowski's 1972 *King, Queen, Knave* starred the would-be Humbert, David Niven (his face a prune of prim pain), as the king; Gina Lollobrigida (a Via Veneto mannequin, all frosted comeliness) as the queen; and John Moulder-Brown (*Deep End*'s obsessive innocent) as the knave. To the Nabokov story, Skolimowski was as faithful as a fishwife. But he went, perversely, for a deeper fidelity. He made the piece coarse, like the manners of the cuckolded husband; inhuman, like the ambitions of the brittle, brutal wife; clumsy, like the hands of the young seducer. Only the poetry was lost in transmutation.

Line 20: his books-into-films

Nabokov authorised several other novels for adaptation and was pleased to itemise them for Alfred Appel: '*Bend Sinister* was done on West German television, an opera based on *Invitation to a Beheading* was shown on West German TV, and my play *The Event* [1938] appeared on Finnish TV.' An adaptation of his first novel, *Maschenka*, played on German TV in 1986. In the past few years, more works have been optioned: *The Defence* for Louis Becker's French company, *Laughter in the Dark* as a French-American coproduction, and 'Mademoiselle O.', a chapter from *Speak, Memory* in which he recalls his family's French governess, recently slated for filming in St. Petersburg.

A few years ago yet another film of *Laughter in the Dark* was proposed, to star Rebecca de Mornay as Margot. The actress finally rejected the Nabokov project – in part because, as Dmitri Nabokov recalled her saying contemptuously, 'The writer isn't even American.'

Line 22: impaler, Vlad

'My characters cringe as I come near them with my whip,' Nabokov told the BBC in 1977. 'I have seen a whole avenue of imagined trees losing their leaves at the threat of my passage.'

Biographers, interviewers and readers cringe as well, imagining a living version of Philippe Halsman's photograph of Nabokov: furrowed brow on high forehead, a cheekbone resting on his fist, the mouth already a bit tired of the clever words it must frame to crush the questions posed by stupid you. It is the 'game face' of a champ at the weigh-in ceremony of his last bout before retiring undefeated. It is a picture of an intelligence utterly assured of itself. Indeed, nowhere in 560 pages of his collected *Letters* does Nabokov admit he has changed his mind. Perhaps he thought it too imposing and delicate a monument to be moved.

Kubrick, a more reclusive chessmaster, is imposing as well. In photographs his high forehead, majestic rumpled curls and ferocious, abstracted stare make him look like a Bronx Beethoven. He rarely leaves his Hertfordshire estate, and when he does venture out to make a film, his imperious reputation envelops him. A 1993 article in the *Daily Telegraph* reported that during the *Full Metal Jacket* shoot, 'At a New Year's Eve party thrown by the crew, the main topic of conversation was how best to murder the director without being detected.' But that was just banter. The loyalty of his main support staff (cinematographer John Alcott, casting director Leon Vitali, costumer Milena Canonero, among many others) suggests that Kubrick is a man worth working for.

Line 25: I intersected with the movies' gaze

Movies are about looking. We sit in the dark, unseen by those we watch. It is a communal snoop, voyeurism raised and intensified into art appreciation. In the film of *Lolita*, Quilty offers Humbert the chance 'to attend executions, how would you like that? Just you there, nobody else. Just watching, watching. You like watching, Captain?'

Traditionally, though, movies have been about men watching women. The camera is a prying eye, demanding and star-struck as it considers female beauty. And because cinema is a series of *moving* pictures, the camera catches female mutability: girls becoming women, accruing radiance, shedding innocence. The camera, in other words, is Humbert, watching Lolita until he erupts in the dark.

Mostly, film is the validation of memory – a moving snapshot, most moving to the man who can possess his little girl in tennis whites only on the inside of his eyelids. As Humbert writes: 'Idiot, triple idiot! I could have filmed her! I would have had her now with me, before my eyes, in the projection room of my pain and despair! ... That I could have had all her strokes, all her enchantments, immortalised in segments of celluloid, makes me moan today in frustration.' Nabokov and Humbert – yes, and Quilty too – wanted to see Lolita in the movies. They knew there were a few things film could capture.

Line 26: As Humbert saw

In any form of art we see what the maker intends us to see. All else we imagine. Reading *Lolita*, a solipsist's memoir, we see everything through Humbert's eyes; there is blood in them, and starlight. The condemned man fills his prison journal with acute, minute descriptions of his world . But he knows a crucial piece is missing: our view of him. 'Imagine me!' he pleads. 'I will not exist if you do not imagine me.'

In the book we have less to imagine about Humbert, for it begins decades before the movie does. The early scenes in the novel provide psychological clues to Humbert's mistreatment of women and desperate ambition to be, among other things, a father to his little girl. Young Humbert's mother is dead ('picnic, lightning') and his promiscuous father is absent ('touring Italy with Mme. de R. and her daughter' – poor daughter!) when, at 13, the lad has a groping, furtive, wondrously convulsive affair with a child his age, Annabel Leigh, the ur-Lolita. They love each other. They are separated. She dies.

Nabokov despised Freud; he believed that psychoanalysis unfairly freed people from a proper sense of responsibility and deprived human personality of its irreducible mystery. Yet *Lolita* offers clues to Humbert's complaint that might rouse a repulsed audience to pity: he is condemned to repeat the sins of his father (heredity); he is doomed by the tragic loss of first passion (environment). Grown Humbert's nympholust could be a symptom of young Humbert's grief sickness; that is why he searches out her avatar in every girl he sees. Lolita, Humbert believes upon meeting her, is 'the same child'.

A film of *Lolita*, especially one constructed in flashback form, might include Humbert's 'backstory'. What it would still lack is a suitable equivalent to Humbert's voice – not the sound of it, not the words, but the unique tone. His prose is in a perpetual state of ecstasy: for Lolita, first and last, but also for whatever he sees and feels. He is aroused by all things, physical, tactile, ethereal, ephemeral; they alight on his erect palp and he comes alive so intensely that his heart could burst. (Which it does.) *Lolita* is rapture rekindled.

Line 28: gilded kitsch

Lolita forges a narrative chain of unrequited lust. Charlotte loves Humbert, who doesn't love her but does love Lolita, who doesn't love him but does love Quilty, who doesn't love her. Charlotte, Humbert, Lolita: each gets to possess the covered body of another, then gets betrayed. As the only unloved person in the progression, Charlotte should be the most poignant. She is not, because *Lolita* is not her story; it attends carefully to the suffering of everyone in the Haze family but her. In character terms, Charlotte is a comic foil. In story terms, she is the gilded kitsch, the useful fool, the one disposable life. So let Charlotte be pretentious, irritating, a bossy lover, a behemoth mom. Let her be, in the film, 'the brainless ba-ba' (though in the novel Humbert applied that epithet to his first wife, Valeria). Charlotte's sins of style will absolve Humbert, in the viewer's mind, of guilt for her death.

In the film we first see Charlotte escorting prospective lodger Humbert up her stairs. Her wardrobe – tight blonde curls, thickish face, cigarette on a stalk, her ample frame hugged by black leotards under a jumper secured with a leopard-skin belt – screams suburban *artiste manquée*. (Later, at her midnight supper for Humbert, Charlotte changes into 'something cozier': a leopard-skin sun suit that makes good on the sexual threat of the belt.) 'Oh, M'sieur,' she says as she leads Humbert on a labyrinthine tracking shot through the house, 'if what you're needing is peace and quiet, I assure you you couldn't get more peace [piece] anywhere!' She puts her hand to her chest in an *oh-naughty-me!* gesture and emits a convivial explosion: part laugh, part cigarette cough, and, in this case, louder than needed to underline the come-hither bawdiness of Madame's little joke.

The tour, from the moment Humbert enters the house until we

see Lolita, extends over four minutes and three shots; and except for a blatantly mismatched cut, the sequence is a finely judged comic set piece. Shelley Winters virtually cha-chas as she sits; she uses the cigarette holder as a Balinese dancer would her cymbals; she stands six inches too close to this stranger and strikes artful poses in the doorway. She is a woman who must make this sale (of herself) to this prospective client (husband). Mason's movements, in reaction, are wondrously constipated. He indulges in evasive chat, raising his eyebrows in a pretence of interest, briefly taking in the expanse of the lady's poitrine (Humbert is impressed but not tempted). His pained eyes scan this prison for any means of escape; at one point he simply walks out of the frame. And Winters keeps talking. Her Charlotte is impervious to the aggression in her body language or to the recoil in Humbert's.

Many contradictions are on display here. Charlotte's Chamber of Commerce banter is undercut by her sexual predations. Her name-dropping of the Great Masters – Dufy, Van Gogh, Monet, Schweitzer, Zhivago, Quilty – can be seen by Humbert as vulgar and by the mass movie audience as snooty; she is too low for the movie's tastes and too high for the moviegoer's. The modern-woman *savoir faire* Charlotte affects is constantly sabotaged by her desperation; she is miserable, she

Charlotte escorting prospective lodger Humbert

knows it, and she probably knows she can't hide it. In her pursuit of Humbert (a man already in love with her daughter), Charlotte is the 'foolish romantic American girl' and Lolita is the mature cynic. Finally, the precision Winters brings to her burlesque of a suburban matron is often overwhelmed by the actress' iconic unsuitability for the role.

In the novel, Humbert at first calls Charlotte 'a weak solution of Marlene Dietrich', and much later hears her described as 'a celebrated actress killed in an airplane crash'. We imagine Lola Lola and Carole Lombard. Instead we get Brooklyn-reared Shirley Schrift, whose gauche, fleshy, whining screen personality begged to be put down. And, so often in movies, she was. As Winters recalls in an autobiography, *Shelley II*, 'I had been strangled by Ronald Colman, drowned by Montgomery Clift, stabbed and drowned by Robert Mitchum, shot by Jack Palance and by Rod Steiger in two different films, and OH YES, overdosed with heroin by Ricardo Montalban.' Charlotte must die, for the tale to progress; and when she dies, no one must care. Winters' job was to make the character memorably disagreeable – to make a strong, bad impression, then get off.

Perhaps life on the set imitated art in the camera. 'Shelley Winters was very difficult,' Oswald Morris recalled, 'wanting to do everything her own way. She was very nearly fired off the film. At one point Kubrick said to me, "I think the lady's gonna have to go" – which would have been very serious, halfway through production. But he'd have got rid of her, he really didn't care about the consequences.' Since Kubrick filmed *Lolita* more or less in sequence, he knew that the Shelley ordeal would be history halfway into shooting.

Winters does appear to be twenty pounds heavier, fifteen decibels higher and ten I.Q. points lower than Charlotte deserves. When she meets Quilty, she dances around him like an elephant cow in heat. In bed with Hum, she is both pouty and calculating, making Humbert a henpecked husband like Elisha Cook, Jr in *The Killing*. And when Charlotte discovers, through Humbert's diary, his loathing for her and his lust for Lolita, Winters brays at such length that the viewer can feel no sympathy – only a sort of wincing pity. Winters' Charlotte is, in sum, everything that Hum, Lo and the moviegoer hate. Which is why her performance is so daring, so right. She played Charlotte true, not to the character, but to the movie. She is the bookend to Quilty: a monster from whom (not *to* whom) a girl might want to flee.

Winters and Lyon are not exactly Charlotte and Lo. But they might be those characters as seen in the distorting eye of Humbert, the casting director of his own fantasy. In this view, Lo-Lyon is the girleen as teen, her figure filled out by a voyeur's roguish appreciation. And Charlotte-Shelley is the perfectly coarse fraufrump, made unappealing both to a nympholept (who believes that all grown women are past their prime) and to typical moviegoers, whose tutelage in the dark has taught them to love many women – but not this one.

Line 29: American fake

Humbert drives up a foggy road and enters Castle Quilty, a haunted house whose ground floor is strewn with the detritus of a blow-out the night before: full ashtrays, empty liquor bottles, a ping-pong table, and, improbably, a harp. There are crates everywhere; the furniture and some *objets d'art* are draped in sheets – if Charles Foster Kane had been a sybarite, this would be his Xanadu. Humbert, a vengeful lover with a gun in his coat pocket, shouts out, 'Quilty. Quilty!' And from the rear of the shot a bottle tumbles off an easy chair. The bottle has been perched on the sleeping head of the mansion's owner, who rises sleepily from the chair, with the sheet as a toga, and proclaims himself, 'Spartacus. You come to free the slaves or some'n?'

Every relationship, with or without gunplay, is a power struggle. And nowhere are the combatants less equal than in a love affair. To love is to be vulnerable, naked; a declaration of love is a confession of weakness. To be loved is to be strong, pampered, armoured in the lover's ardour. The withholding of love is such a valuable weapon; it forces the lover to keep trying to scale the frosty peak of the beloved's indifference. Like danger, indifference is an aphrodisiac to a lover on the make. The challenge is both moral ('I will reform the Other') and monumental ('I will make the Other love me!'). And it tends to end in humiliating defeat, since emotions of the heart or loins are rarely susceptible to siege.

So Humbert is stronger than Charlotte, because she loves him and he only tolerates her. Lolita is stronger than Humbert, at least as soon as this European connoisseur develops a tender love for her. Clare Quilty – the ultimate unlover, the brutal and wily user, the American faker, with a native love (shared by Lolita) of pranks – is strongest of

all. Strong because of the mystery that envelops his venality.

Nothing is clear about Clare Quilty, except that he is clearly guilty. Like Conan Doyle's Moriarty or Stoker's Dracula, Nabokov's Quilty is a criminal mastermind frequently spoken of but rarely seen. In the book he has only one major scene (his death) and a few spectral cameos. He dwells in the shadows. He is known by his pernicious effect on others. We sense his presence, infer his sexiness and cunning, from the way he makes Lolita feel warm and Humbert feel sick. But when Quilty finally surfaces, he seems as unremarkable in appearance and demeanour as many a great seducer or madman: there is nothing special about him except, perhaps, a fey, slurred wickedness. He is Lolita without the elfin charm, Humbert without the great shuddering soul.

In the novel and film Quilty, whose Uncle Ivor is the local dentist, had visited Ramsdale to address Charlotte's literary club and had an affair with her. There he had noticed Lolita. Indeed, he may have been the girls deflowerer. 'Sensitive gentlewomen of the jury,' the book's Humbert pleads, 'I was not even her first lover.' He means us to believe, as he wants to, that the culprit was Charlie, the gonadal geek at Lo's summer camp. But how much more poetically apt if Quilty were Lolita's seducer, first and forever. If so Humbert would be absolved of the crime of ruining his stepdaughter, even as he was made to realise that at no time in their courtship had he been anything but second best, a stand-in for the genuine evil goods. 'Do you want to die standing up or sitting down?' Humbert asks Quilty in the movie, just before he shoots him. The doomed man dons boxing gloves and says, 'I want to die like a champion.' And that is how Quilty dies: as the champion of Lolita's unquenchable love-letch.

To incarnate this chameleon Kubrick chose Peter Sellers, who had secured international recognition playing three roles in *The Mouse That Roared* (1959). Sellers was often compared with Alec Guinness, who had played all eight members of the D'Ascoyne family in *Kind Hearts and Coronets*. But Guinness had honed his craft on the stage, inhabiting characters designed to make sense throughout an evening's entertainment, and appearing in multiple roles only as an occasional lark. Sellers was a product of radio sketch comedy, in which the actor makes a quick satirical strike, then moves on to the next target. The most brilliant mimic among the regular cast of BBC radio's *The Goon Show*, he had created hundreds of eccentric voices, including such luminaries as Winston Churchill, the Queen and Lew Grade. In his early films Sellers did more of these turns, playing types whose character, in so far as they had any, proceeded from their regional accents. Further, the two performers were opposite types: Guinness thin, wispy, able to play the middle-class Englishman from a red-brick university whose intelligence outstrips his station; Sellers thick, Germanic, able to play men less brilliant than they thought themselves. He might have been destined for supporting-man roles – as he was in *The Ladykillers*, playing his dull-witted thug to Guinness' gentle-genius villain – if *The Mouse That Roared* hadn't given him the innocent hero to play amid the two other, Goonier parts.

Kubrick adored the actor's fertile wit, here and later; he shot *Dr Strangelove* in Britain primarily because Sellers, whom, the director considered the crucial performer in the project, was kept at home by his divorce case. On *Lolita*, Sellers worked with Kubrick and Harris on Quilty's peculiar American accent, which was based on the speech patterns of Norman Granz, a Los Angeles-born jazz impresario (Verve Records, Jazz at the Philharmonic) who had been employed as an editor at MGM in the 40s; at the film-makers' request, Granz tape-recorded a few of Quilty's speeches for Sellers to study and imitate. Perhaps Granz did sound like Sellers' Quilty ('Aaaah, that huuuuut!' he shouts when he is hurt). But in the ricochet cadences of Sellers' delivery, in his nervous repetitions, in the wild range of his allusions, in the competitiveness and defensiveness, in the sense of a performer who is too hip for the room but whose most demanding audience is himself – in the pit of Sellers' improvisations one can hear echoes of a New York comedian who might have been a great Quilty: Lenny Bruce.

On *Lolita*, Sellers had a freedom of interpretation that few actors have enjoyed, with Kubrick or any other director: he was encouraged to devise, not only his own character, but much of his own dialogue. 'The most interesting scenes,' says Morris, 'were the ones with Peter Sellers, which were total improvisations. They'd roughly block it out, go upstairs and leave me to light it, then come down with, for instance, the table tennis scene. There was nothing like that in the script, it was just off the cuff.' So Sellers' four major scenes with Mason – at the Quilty mansion, at the Enchanted Hunters, in Humbert's Beardsley home, and in a phone call to Humbert's motel room – have the feeling of skits, showcases for the star; and some of them extend past the requirements of the story or the humour. Mason found Kubrick 'so besotted with the genius of Peter Sellers that he seemed never to have enough of him'.

Quilty is in three short sequences with people other than Humbert; each time he is with his sepulchral companion, Vivian Darkbloom. They are at the summer dance, where Charlotte reintroduces herself to Quilty and whispers a reminder of their tryst. 'Listen. Listen, din you have a dawda? Din you have a dawda with a lovely name? Yeah, a lovely, what was it now, a lovely lyrical lilting like, ah [...] Lolita, diminutive of Dolores, the tears and the roses.' At the Enchanted Hunters, just before Humbert and Lolita arrive, Quilty and Darkbloom are at the front desk with the oleaginous night man, George Swine, a kindred soul; Quilty and Swine, an actor, are auditioning each other's libidos. And at a high school production of his play *The Lady Who Loved Lightning*, in which Lolita stars as an Ariel angel, Quilty instructs a Swine-ish aide to 'go and get some Type A Kodachrome' – for Quilty's art movies, no doubt.

Humbert, though he shares the playwright's fondness for cute young things, can never be Quilty; the professor has a little gnawing humanity left inside. He is a better Quilty, or a lesser one – that is what Quilty thinks, and that is why he thinks Humbert must be destroyed. Also for the sport, and the fun of it. So in Sellers' scenes with Mason, he exercises Quilty's ingenuity. Here, we see Quilty at work: the playwright, who knows 'all about tragedy and comedy and fantasy', is toying with Humbert as he might with a character in one of his more devious fictions.

At the hotel, where he quickly notices that Humbert has the same lecherous eyes for Lolita that he has, Quilty impersonates a state trooper, putting the first whisper of a threat in Humbert's mind. In the Humbert home, where Quilty may just have enjoyed the corrupting of a minor, he masquerades as the school psychiatrist, Dr Zempf, trying to persuade a naive dad that his daughter is a growing girl ('Well, Doktor Humbarts, to you she's still za liddle girl what is cradled in za arms. But to doze boys over dare at Beardsley High, she is a lovely girl, you know, mit mit mit mit mit de *sving*, you know, und zat jazz') and that she should be allowed to appear in the school play – Quilty's play, the private rehearsals for which will occupy author and ingénue for many a lurid afternoon. At the motel, Humbert receives an anonymous phone call from a man asking about 'the bizarre rumours that have been

PETER SELLERS
092-P25A

Studio portrait of Peter Sellers

circulating about you and that lovely remarkable girl you've been travelling around with. ... I wonder if you'd be prepared to give our investigator the report, Professor, on your current sex life. If any.'

Here, Sellers is back on radio, teasing his audience with a funny voice and a naughty trick. You can fairly hear him sniggering under his breath (while, giggling next to Quilty, in a phone booth on the way to a swell honeymoon, must be Lolita). He is a tiresome cartoon in his Dr Zempf role, with bottle-cap eyeglasses recalling Dr Cyclops and a music-hall German accent prefiguring Dr Strangelove; the scene goes on too long. The Enchanted Hunters riff is closer to inspiration, with Sellers rushing through a kind of Noo Yawk rap while his lids blink neurotically over surprisingly wistful eyes. But the opening scene shows the best that Sellers, and maybe the movie, can offer. He begins as a bleary drunk. In the next nine minutes we see a mind wake up, exercise its wiles with accelerating desperation, and finally soar, like old grey mad Nijinsky, into the orgasm of fatal pain.

Line 34: René Clair

In his Berlin days Nabokov was a frequent moviegoer. He respected certain serious films (*The Last Laugh*, *The Hands of Orlac*), 'and I loved the French films of René Clair – *Sous les Toits de Paris*, *Le Million*, *À Nous la Liberté* – a new world, a new trend in cinema.' Best of all were the clowns: Chaplin, Keaton, Lloyd, Laurel and Hardy, the Marx Brothers. Decades later, for Appel, he could quote in detail the stateroom scene from *A Night at the Opera* and map out with precise delight every false turn of the garden labyrinth in *A Chump at Oxford*.

Even more, though, he loved to hate movies. Brian Boyd, the novelist's premier biographer, cites a recollection by Iosif Hessen, editor of the émigré magazine *Rul*: 'For Sirin [Nabokov's pseudonym], there seemed no greater pleasure than to single out intentionally an inept American film. The more casually stupid it was, the more he would choke and literally shake with laughter, to the point where on occasion he would have to leave the hall.'

Appel cautions that we should not confuse derision with what he believes to be the raucous enjoyment Nabokov took in low comedy and melodrama. The author might have been shaking with surprise at some creaky bit of business, or with astonishment at his realisation that the old tricks still worked.

Lines 39–40: blind to their huge doubles

It is said that people, while watching movies, lose themselves in the picture fictions. Nabokov, in his novels, says that people lose themselves by not watching closely enough. His characters stumble into theatres and past billboards, missing the clues the author has laid out for them like road signs: DETOUR, CHILDREN AT PLAY, DANGEROUS CURVES AHEAD. Albinus in *Laughter in the Dark*, and Martha in *King, Queen, Knave*, are too busy careering after their obsessions to notice these signs. They'll crash and die.

Line 42 (1): posh lustre

'*Poshlost*', philistine vulgarity, occupies . . . a central place in Nabokov's mind,' Boyd writes. 'It can cover everything from a trite advertisement to the atrocities committed in Lenin's name or Hitler's ... from the harshest cruelty to the insensitivity of sham art, pseudo-refinement, fake sentimentality.' In 1958, Nabokov defined philistines as 'ready-made souls in a plastic bag'. But he could be tolerant of philistine blinkers and energised by the excesses of *poshlost*, even as he was once convulsed by the glamorous banalities of bad Hollywood films. In the axiom of Nabokov's Afterword to *Lolita*: 'Nothing is more exhilarating than philistine vulgarity.'

Line 42 (b): Metro

How did they ever make a film of *Lolita* at Metro-Goldwyn-Mayer? And why did they – Kubrick and Harris – make it in England?

Twenty-five or even five years earlier, the pairing of Nabokov's pre-teen feline with Leo the Lion would have been inconceivable. Dolores Haze was no sibling to Dorothy Gale, and Humbert Humbert's Ramsdale was in a different galaxy from Judge Hardy's Carvel. Louis B. Mayer, boss of the company from its founding in 1924 until his ousting in 1951, ensured that MGM was the 'family values' studio, when that phrase could still be uttered with a straight face. Irving Thalberg, Metro production chief from 1924 until his early death in 1936, saw feature films as chic merchandise: fifty units a year to be moved along the assembly line by the highest-paid dreamfitters in the nation. The notion of a maverick like Kubrick directing a project like *Lolita*, 5,000 miles away at Associated British Studios, would have been dismissed by Mayer or Thalberg in a curt memo.

By the early 1960s, though, the Old Guard was gone and the grandest of Hollywood studios was primarily a distributor of foreign films. Of the twenty-seven features MGM released in 1962, only eleven were uniquely US productions. Among these were the year's box-office champ, *How the West Was Won*, and the most expensive film to that time, *Mutiny on the Bounty* – on which Carol Reed, Graham Greene's frequent collaborator, was replaced as director by Lewis Milestone, the collaborator Nabokov once wished for (*see note to line 58*).

The rest of the slate represented international commercial movie-making of the period, including three Italian sex-and-pects epics of the *Hercules* school (one was *Son of Spartacus*, a knock-off of the Kubrick spectacular). The other ten were British films, modern equivalents of the 'quota quickies' of the 30s. This surge in product was inspired partly by the international appeal of Hammer horror films and Peter Sellers comedies. Eric Sykes, a writer for *The Goon Show*, starred in two farces released by the company. Sellers graced a pair of British MGM comedies as well: *The Dock Brief* (in the US, *Trial and Error*), John Mortimer's very dry run for the Rumpole series; and *Lolita*.

All right, but why film *Lolita* at Elstree? Money, mostly. While Kubrick was shooting *Spartacus*, Harris visited Europe to secure funds for *Lolita*. He found them, he says, quicker than he thought possible, when Ken Hyman, a school chum, took Harris to lunch with Ken's father Elliot. The Hymans owned Seven Arts, a Canadian production outfit that later bought Warner Bros. 'What do you want, kid?' the senior Hyman asked Harris. He replied, 'A million dollars.' 'You got it.' Harris signed the contract, which contained a clause that the Hymans could not touch a frame of the film. He also knew that if the film were made in England, it would qualify for Eady benefits. In a trice, *Lolita* became a British film – though it was technically Swiss, since the two companies Kubrick and Harris created to produce the picture, Anya Productions (named after one of Kubrick's daughters) and Transworld Pictures, were registered in Switzerland.

Line 48: recruit for Quilty's porn

At the Duk Duk Ranch, an artists' enclave in the Southwest to which Quilty had taken Lo after her escape from Humbert, the playwright encouraged his protégée to engage in 'Oh, weird, filthy, fancy things. I mean, he had two girls and two boys, and three or four men, and the idea was for all of us to tangle in the nude while an old woman took movie pictures.' (Lolita's choice of the word 'fancy' is inspired.)

Later in the novel (early in the film), Quilty informs Humbert that he is the author of 'fifty-two successful scenarios'. The book adds this helpful footnote: 'I have made private movies out of *Justine* and other eighteenth-century sexcapades.'

Duck Ranch, we learn from Boyd, is a spread the Nabokovs rented in August 1951, just after visiting Telluride, Colorado (*see note to line 90*). *Duk* is 'an obscene Oriental word for copulation'. This and other pertinent keys, passwords and combinations may be found in Appel's *The Annotated Lolita*.

Line 50: movie hack

'By nature I am no dramatist,' wrote Nabokov, introducing his published screenplay of *Lolita*. 'I am not even a hack scenarist; but if I had given as much of myself to the stage or the screen as I have to the kind of writing which serves a triumphant life sentence between the pages of a book, I would have advocated and applied a system of total tyranny, directing the play or the picture myself, choosing settings and costumes, terrorising the actors, mingling with them in the bit part of guest, or ghost, prompting them, and, in a word, pervading the entire show with the will and art of one individual.'

He sounds like the later Stanley Kubrick.

Line 51: once I was a picture writer

Within a decade of the Bolshevik revolution, some 200,000 Russians had teemed into Berlin. Nabokov lived there from 1923 to 1937, completing nine novels, several plays and many poems (all in Russian). But he was always on the lookout to make a living.

To Nabokov, then, movies held out the lure of economic survival.

By 1924 he was writing movie scripts, hoping modestly for a $1,000–3,000 pay-off per script. But even he realised the task demanded at least a craftsman's dedication. 'I have understood,' he wrote that year, 'that one must really create for the cinema, and that's not so easy.' Selling his work would be even harder: none of Nabokov's Berlin scripts became films. Nor did a project, *Hotel Magique*, possibly an early sketch for *The Real Life of Sebastian Knight*, in which, a decade later, he tried to interest a Parisian producer named Dostokiyan. (So attests Boyd, though the producer's name sounds like a joke on Nabokov's favourite bugbear, Fyodor 'Old Dusty' Dostoevsky.)

Line 54: a movie-extra crowd

Nabokov was ever a gifted performer: behind the lectern, on stage, and in films. His courses at Cornell attracted 400 students, rapt with the professor's star quality. As a young man in Yalta, Nabokov had played Fritz Lobheimer, the indiscreet dragoon, in a production of Schnitzler's *Liebelei*. As a poet in Berlin he was as famous for his reading as for his writing. 'I always had a friendly audience,' he expansively told his severest critic and biographer, Andrew Field, 'being a man of *tremendous* charm when I was young.' Could the camera catch that élan, or that ego? Nabokov says it tried. Like so many other Russians in Germany, he eked out his living with occasional work as an extra for the thriving Russian émigré film companies, possibly including Ivan Mozhukhin's. In a 1925 letter to his mother, the penurious young poet spoke of working from eight to five on a movie set. 'The next day,' as Andrew Field paraphrases the note, 'his eyebrows were still blackened from the makeup that wouldn't come off, and he was still seeing bright spots in front of his eyes from the blinding lights.'

Line 56 (a): As Hitchcock did

In the introduction to his *Lolita* screenplay, Nabokov recalled crowds at the film's New York premiere peering 'into my car hoping to glimpse James Mason but finding only the placid profile of a stand-in for Hitchcock'. In stature the two men were no twins – Hitchcock a melon, Nabokov a banana that ripened into a pear. But both had the character actor's prerequisite: they were perfect 'types', visual correlatives of the evil-imp auteur and the imperious author

Other similarities abound. Both artists worked for the most part in a narrow genre, the sex-and-murder thriller, with baroque and spectacular results. Both created worlds – unique, frightening, familiar – so indelibly that, by appending an 'ian' to their names, one may define not only their output but that of their imitators. And both enjoyed refining their old works. Hitchcock remade *The Man Who Knew Too Much* once, and revisited the nightmare man-on-the-run landscape of *The 39 Steps* several times. Nabokov spent his last fifteen years adapting his Russian novels into English (and translating *Lolita* into Russian), while writing his last four English-language novels. As John Updike remarked at the time, Nabokov's oeuvre was growing at both ends.

In 1964, Hitchcock sounded out Nabokov about writing a film script. The director provided two story outlines: one a romance about a defector and his fiancée (*Torn Curtain*, eventually); the other about a family of thieves who work in a hotel. Nabokov found both ideas 'very interesting'. He thought the first would require more knowledge of US intelligence agencies than he possessed, but said that the second 'is quite acceptable to me. Given a complete freedom (as I assume you intend to give me) I think I could turn it into a screenplay.' Give complete freedom to a writer? Hitchcock must have thought the novelist was daft. Nothing ever came of their proposed collaboration.

The work of any two authors may be found to intersect, felicitously if fortuitously. Here's one such juncture, from *King, Queen, Knave* (1928): an eerie, indeed psycho-kinetic anticipation of the climax to a 1960 Hitchcock film. Franz, the knave, has heard his landlord, Enricht, conversing with an unseen woman in the flat below; one day he goes downstairs and knocks on their bedroom door. The rest of the scene is rendered in screenplay shorthand: 'No answer. He pushed the door and stepped in. The old woman whose face he had never seen sat with her back to him in her usual place. "I'm leaving; I want to say good-bye," he said, advancing toward the armchair. There was no woman at all – only a grey wig stuck to a stick and a knitted shawl. He knocked the whole dusty contraption to the floor. Old Enricht came out from behind a screen. He was stark naked and had a paper fan in his hand. "You no longer exist, Franz Bubendorf," he said dryly, indicating the door with a fan.'

Line 56 (b): Vivian Darkbloom

Nabokov's signature, like Hitchcock's, can of course be read like a palimpsest in every flourish of his art. But also like Hitchcock, he enjoyed hiding, mostly for the pleasure of those who would seek him. Vivian Darkbloom, one of many anagrams for Vladimir Nabokov that surface in his novels (others were Vivian Bloodmark, Dorian Vivalcomb, Vivian Calmbrood and Blavdak Vinomori) was the drag in which he masqueraded as Clare Quilty's mistress. For a time, Nabokov timidly considered publishing *Lolita* under this pseudoplume or nom de nymph. In the 1974 *Lolita* screenplay Quilty says of Vivian, 'Her name looks like an anagram.'

Line 58: Milestone

In early 1924 Nabokov wrote a short story, 'The Potato Elf', with the familiar themes of paedophilia, cuckoldry and revenge: horned conjurer fakes death tò punish wife for having an affair with a dwarf who is often mistaken for an eight-year-old boy. Shortly after writing the story, he revised it into a screenplay, called *The Love of a Dwarf*. Now imagine that this movie-script message in a bottle washed up near the Santa Monica Pier and elicited the interest of Lewis Milestone, who said he might bring its writer to Hollywood to work on other scenarios. The Depression then intervened, according to Nabokov. But the author was encouraged to offer *Camera Obscura* to Milestone, and then *Despair* – he thought some technical wizardy could solve the problem of representing a double on screen. Again his hopes were dashed. Twenty-eight years, three countries and several careers would intervene before Nabokov would go Hollywood.

Line 59: my camera shuttered

Someone was interested in turning *Camera Obscura* into a movie. 'In the middle Thirties a German actor whose name was Fritz Kortner, a most famous and gifted artist of his day [*Backstairs*, *The Hands of Orlac*, *Warning Shadows*, *Pandora's Box*], wanted to make a film of *Camera Obscura*,' Nabokov told Appel in 1970. 'I went to London to see him, nothing came of it, but a few years later another firm, this one in Paris, bought an option which ended in a blind alley too.'

By 1939, when he wrote 'The Enchanter', Nabokov was forty and broke. An old friend, Savely Kyandzhuntsev, gave him 1,000 francs a month, partly from the profits of a cinema he owned. It was the most money Nabokov had yet made from pictures.

Line 61: a nymphet kissed

In two-and-a-half hours of *Lolita* there are but eight kisses. Most are as chaste as a Carmelite's lips. In order:

> Charlotte and Humbert are playing chess. Lo, in a nightgown, enters the room, kisses her mother and Hum 'g'night', cheek to cheek. To the lodger, the girl's intonation carries a gram more emotional weight; her voice is perhaps half an octave lower.

> At the summer dance, John Farlow, Charlotte's free-loving neighbour, plants a social kiss on her cheek, and his wife Jean does the same on Hum's brow.

> That night at home, as Charlotte attempts to seduce Humbert, she kisses and embraces him. Lolita, they discover, is watching.

> To divert Charlotte from thoughts of suicide, Hum leads her to bed and kisses her.

> Receiving him as her hospital visitor just before she is to desert him, Lo allows Humbert to kiss her on the cheek as he enters and leaves. To permit a kiss on the mouth, which she averts from his lips both times, would signal betrayal of her imminent abductor and ever true love, Clare Quilty.

The other glancing physical intimacies between man and maid chart the blooming and festering of their affair. Before being driven to summer camp, Lo rushes upstairs and hugs Hum, saying, 'Don't forget me'; it is all he needs to be her slave for life. Hovering above his cot in the Enchanted Hunters, she rubs his face, plays hand

5 8   Charlotte embraces Humbert; Lolita is watching

games and whispers in his ear the venereal game she wants to teach him. In a motel, as he consoles poor sobbing orphan Lo, Hum caresses her hair (dad to daughter) before she curls in his lap (she's too big for that gesture). He paints her toenails as they pursue an argument that Lo, of course, wins. She leaves a telephone booth, in which she has called Quilty, and allows Humbert to hold her hands. On the road her sleeping head rests on his shoulder. Later, in the car, she permits Hum to feel her forehead, which is fevered (for Quilty). Four years later, wracked by her confession, he grabs her wrists, then sobbingly asks her to leave with him. She touches his prayerful hands with a little pity and absolution.

The one forthright come-on in the movie is when stepfather and camper are driving towards the Enchanted Hunters. Daddy Humbert must have stopped caring for poor Lo, she says with that CinemaScope smirk. Why? 'Well, you haven't even kissed me yet, have you?' *Zooooooom* goes Humbert's Melmoth sedan into the distance. The car has a roaring motor, even if the movie's Hum doesn't. And the movie Lolita is willing to entertain her old beau's terms of endearment – but on her own terms.

Line 63: censors

'My poor *Lolita* is having a rough time,' Nabokov wrote to Graham Greene in 1956, when the novel had been published only as a two-volume paperback from the Olympia Press. 'The pity is that if I had made her a boy, or a cow, or a bicycle, philistines might never have flinched. On the other hand, Olympia Press informs me that amateurs (amateurs!) are disappointed with the tame turn my story takes in the second volume, and do not buy it.'

Four US publishing houses had turned down *Lolita* in 1954. The following year the Olympia Press, Maurice Girodias' Paris publishing house specialising in soft-core sex books (as well as works by Beckett, Genet and Burroughs), issued a first printing of 5,000 copies, which quickly sold out. A rave review by Greene stoked outrage in Britain. According to Edward de Grazia in his history of censorship, *Girls Lean Back Everywhere*, the British Home Office 'pressed' the French Ministry of the Interior to put the screws on Girodias; and on 20 December 1956 the Paris police banned *Lolita*. It stayed banned there for two years. The book was published without incident in the US in 1958 and in Britain in 1959.

Such pressure could not be ignored by the young American director, who, within two years, was putting some of this 'sheer unrestrained pornography' on film in a studio outside London. And if Kubrick had put it out of his mind, John Trevelyan, OBE, might have taken pains to remind him. Trevelyan, then secretary of the industry-financed British Board of Film Censors, was empowered to pass or fail all films for exhibition in Britain, and to determine which part of the public might see them. His role, as Alexander Walker described it in *The Celluloid Sacrifice* (1966), was far-ranging. 'If invited to do so, [Trevelyan] will pass an opinion on a subject, vet a script for trouble spots, visit the set for the shooting of a tricky scene, even sit in at the screening of the partially finished film before he "officially" receives it.'

Instead, then, of the Hollywood production code, the Legion of Decency, and any number of local censorship agencies in the US, Kubrick had one man to please and appease. So Trevelyan became a collaborator in the making of *Lolita*. 'The censor saw Nabokov's screenplay ahead of shooting,' writes Walker; 'and it was immediately clear to Trevelyan that the scenarist and the director had resolved many of his own apprehensions, often brilliantly.' Lolita was already a girl of 14 or so, not twelve; the sexual couplings described in the book were literally reduced to whispers in the film. The film-makers having done so much of his work for him, Trevelyan pressed only one major point. In the script, when Humbert offers his theory of nymphets (*see note to line 9*), his narration was to be illustrated, according to Walker, 'by quick-cutting through a series of nymphet-type adolescents – schoolgirls, store girls, cinema usherettes, etc. . . . [Trevelyan] did not relish the risk of putting Nabokov's possibly stimulating theory of nymphets so directly into people's minds. Moreover, it offered a dangerous generalisation from a case history that censors would prefer audiences to believe was rare and specific to Humbert Humbert. The sequence did not appear in the film.'

Lolita was rated 'X' and released with the British censor's deadpan blessing: 'This is to Certify that "Lolita" has been Passed for Exhibition when no child under 16 is present.' In the US, children were also forbidden. Sue Lyon wanted to attend the film's Hollywood premiere, but she couldn't get in.

'*Lolita* is not about sex, but about love,' wrote Lionel Trilling. 'This makes it unique in my experience of contemporary novels.'

Trilling was surely teasing; he wanted his readers to know that *Lolita* was not *only* about sex. But whatever else the novel is about, it is surely about sex – sex as pleasure and punishment, as fantasy, as power tool, as reason for living and cue for despair. The author, a word magician whose novels were part treasure hunt, part cryptic crossword (among many other parts), would be expected to lace his 'Confessions of a White Widowed Male' with sexual allusions, if only as a reward for the diligent reader. A secret smile must have creased the face of the Ivy League professor as he penned this 'dirty book' – at once the form's parody, refutation and apotheosis.

Humbert's early pursuit of Lolita follows the contours of pornographic prose, though the silhouette has elegant shadings. In Ramsdale, Lolita would perch in his lap, 'while I crushed out against her left buttock the last throb of the longest ecstasy man or monster had ever known'. Just before she seduces him in the hotel, Hum has visions of his drugged concubine: 'Naked, except for one sock and her charm bracelet, spread-eagled on the bed where my philter had felled her … her honey-brown body … presented to me its pale breastbuds; in the rosy lamplight, a little pubic floss glistened on its plump hillock.' You can always count on a pervert for a fancy prose style.

'One of the basic problems with the book,' said Kubrick to American reviewer, Joseph Gelmis, 'and with the film even in its modified form, is that the main narrative interest boils down to the question "Will Humbert get Lolita into bed?" And you find in the book that, despite the brilliant writing, the second half has a drop in narrative interest after he does.' Kubrick's take on *Lolita* is a bit like that of *A Clockwork Orange*'s Alex on the Bible: 'I didn't so much like the latter part of the book, which is more preachy-talking than fighting and the old in-out.'

Well, maybe. In *Lolita* the novelty of paedophiliac seduction does cede to two more traditional literary tropes: a detective story (Who is that man following Hum and Lo?) and a love story (Can a dirty old dinosaur such as Humbert see past the girl's ephemeral allure into her shattered soul and find his heart's quest there?). And browsers for familiar prurience may drop out altogether in the novel's second half, as they realise that Nabokov is not only deflecting prurient expectation but punishing it by revealing Humbert as the monster he has always jauntily proclaimed himself to be. Here Humbert's steamy dreaminess evaporates and his sexual villainy flourishes.

The movie Humbert is a pitiful, pliable creature in the second half; he has won his hard desire only to find that Lo has cast him as a powerless stepdad, a henpecked spouse, a whiny cuckold. He is her slave: the pathetic Professor Unrath to an infant Lola Lola. He cooks, he shops, he frets; he is (only this noble, obsolete term will do) a wife. The novel's Humbert is a slave master, revelling in his sham roles of father, lover and drill sergeant. To encourage her to perform in his pageants, he would bribe her, threaten her with reform school, or simply overwhelm her. Hum portrays himself as the stern, loving parent when, 'thrusting my fatherly fingers deep into Lo's hair from behind, and then gently but firmly clasping them around the nape of her neck, I would lead my reluctant pet to our small home for a quick connection before dinner.' Towards the end Hum and Lo are no longer two lovers (even in his mind), or a sick burlesque of father and child. Theirs is a marriage, of great brutality and desperation.

'*Lolita* is a tragedy,' Nabokov wrote in 1956. 'Pornography is not an image plucked out of context. Pornography is an attitude and an intuition. The tragic and the obscene exclude one another.' Further, this is at heart a novel of redemption. It is about a lust that matures, under fire, to love. The reader must know Humbert's capacity for evil to appreciate, finally, the abyss whose walls he heroically climbs.

Line 65 (a): the child

Lolita *is* a child; Humbert is her guardian and defiler. Most sexual abuse of children is the handiwork of men, twice or many times older than they, who are familiar figures of authority. Little wonder, then, that some readers of *Lolita* view Humbert, for all his pretty words and sanctified masochism, as simply a child molester. And in Nabokov, who offers such tiddles as 'the first appearance of pigmented pubic hair (11.2 years)', they see a pervert's apologist, if not his double.

But Nabokov makes no excuse for this protagonist, any more than he does for Albinus or Dreyer or Hermann. He presents Humbert as a creature at one, not only with Dante (who 'fell madly in love with his Beatrice when she was nine') and Petrarch (whose Laura was 'a fair-haired nymphet of twelve') and Poe (whose 'Annabel Lee' is reborn in Humbert's idyllic youth), but with the long line of warped souls who would lock a child in the dank basement of their fantasies, who would betray, imprison, sodomise and leave for dead a kid whose only crime was to trust Daddy, or Uncle John, or the bachelor neighbour.

Line 65 (b): and me rich

For most of Nabokov's life, fiction was a fool's vocation. He had survived for thirty-five years by teaching: tennis, English as a second language, comparative literature. At first the publication of *Lolita* earned him only recriminations with Girodias. In 1957 he confessed that he probably could not afford to consult a lawyer on the Girodias dispute: 'I am absolutely penniless at this moment and owe my bank 800 dollars.'

From poverty to notoriety: it's the American way. *Lolita* had transformed the author, known only to *New Yorker* readers and Cornell liberal arts students, into a sudden star, with all of celebrity's powerful perquisites. By 1959 he had acquired as his advisers a top law firm (Paul Weiss) and a legendary showbiz agent, Irving 'Swifty' Lazar, who happily informed Nabokov that *Lolita* was the first book since *Gone With the Wind* to sell 100,000 copies in its first three weeks in US bookstores.

No less than Humbert, Nabokov was a possessive parent of Lolita. He dismissed the first movie suitor to come calling after the novel's US publication; indeed, it seemed as if he was immune to the idea. Lewis M. Allen, a producer of off-Broadway plays and later of off-Hollywood films (*The Connection, The Balcony, The Lord of the Flies, Fahrenheit 451*), made a bid within a fortnight of publication. 'His offer does not appeal to me at all,' Nabokov wrote to his publisher in September 1958. 'For one thing, my supreme, and in fact only, interest in these motion picture contracts is money. I don't give a damn for what they call "art". Moreover, I would vet the use of a real child. Let them find a dwarfess.' Yet nine days later he was agreeing to terms offered by Harris and Kubrick. He also sold them *Laughter in the Dark*, which appealed to the film-makers because of its similarity to *Lolita* and which they ultimately rejected as a movie project for the same reason.

Over the next few years Nabokov would rebuff what he saw as

exploitation of his property, such as a request from the esteemed Hollywood tunesmith Harry Warren (*You Must Have Been a Beautiful Baby*; *The Girl You Used to Be*) to compose a *Lolita* theme. And he would guard against unlicensed use of the word 'nymphet'. He alerted Kubrick to news that Alberto Lattuada was planning to direct 'an adaptation of Vladimir Nabokov's novel' to be called *The Little Nymph*. Perhaps Nabokov's vigilance wore him out. In the spring of 1960, he wrote to a friend, 'I feel bored and dejected, despite *Lolita*'s noisy triumphs.'

Work on the *Lolita* screenplay earned Nabokov $100,000.

Line 66: my movie-writing itch

'In 1959 I was invited to Hollywood by Harris and Kubrick,' Nabokov told reporters on the *Queen Elizabeth* in 1962 as he sailed to New York for the film's première, 'but after several consultations I decided I did not want to do it. A year later, in Lugano, I received a telegram from them urging me to reconsider my decision. In the meantime a kind of script had somehow taken shape in my imagination so that actually I was glad they had repeated their offer. I travelled once more to Hollywood, and there, under the jacarandas, worked for six months on the thing. Turning one's novel into a movie script is rather like making a series of sketches for a painting that has long ago been finished and framed. I composed new scenes and speeches in an effort to safeguard a *Lolita* acceptable to me. I knew that if I did not write the script somebody else would, and I also knew that at best the end product in such cases is less of a blend than a collision of interpretations.'

Which is the very phrase to describe Nabokov's several reactions to the film. He saw *Lolita* and, to judge from a Véra Nabokov letter to his cousin, a month later, he liked it: 'Vladimir had been worrying about the picture but already after the preview ... he felt completely reassured. The picture might have been somewhat different had he made it himself but it certainly was excellent anyway and contained nothing whatsoever that he could find offensive, false or in bad taste. He ... even found some of the deviations from his script were very fortunate.'

Yet in his introduction to the screenplay Nabokov says a screening revealed to him 'that only ragged odds and ends of my script had been used. ... Most of the scenes were not really better than the ones I had so carefully composed for Kubrick, and I keenly regretted the waste of my time while admiring Kubrick's fortitude in enduring for six months the evolution and infliction of a useless product.'

The useless and unseemly product that Nabokov inflicted here was rancour. Yet he was leashing himself, if Andrew Field is to be trusted: 'He fought with Stanley Kubrick to snatch back the original filmscript of *Lolita* for publication. He got the rights on very strict conditions that he was not allowed to say anything derogatory about Kubrick's film either in writing or verbally and was, moreover, not to conduct himself badly in public situations. Nabokov exploded with laughter as he told me about the alleged clause, which meant, he said, that he "wasn't permitted to screw a cow in a public square".' According to Boyd, Kubrick made Nabokov wait a year before allowing him to publish the screenplay.

The version Nabokov published in 1974 was substantially revised and condensed from this script. If the early version was as prodigal as *Greed* (Nabokov's comparison), the published one is a contentious, puckish fantasia. It may have included, or rejected, scenes used in the film. This *Lolita*, shot as written, would have consumed about four hours of screen time; Kubrick's ran, or ambled, 152 minutes.

The published script begins as the film does, last scene first, with Humbert tracking Clare to his lair, though without the dialogue that Kubrick and Sellers improvised from the book. The rest is a pungent distillation of the novel, including episodes of Humbert's enchanted youth (with the ur-Lolita Annabel Leigh) and his first unhappy marriage (to the un-Lolita Valeria). It expands on the middle section of the novel, in which Lo and her stepfather drive across country.

If Kubrick came close to breaking Nabokov's heart, it was probably not because the film didn't precisely replicate the book but because Nabokov had been at such pleasant pains to exercise his talents on movie-making. His screenplay is much less stagebound and hidebound than the movie. His camera is a lithe, curious creature. It 'glides around' and 'dips into'. 'With a shudder [it] withdraws.' Two pre-teen hands, a boy's and a girl's, meet – 'a pretty scene for the subtle camera'. Like a latterday Lubitsch, a vaulting voyeur, the Nabokamera peers into one hotel bedroom window after another, sliding down drainpipes, tiptoeing on air to spy vivid vignettes. Why can't the *caméra-stylo* be as subtle and supple as a novelist's pen? Why can't a piece of furniture have a mind of its own?' 'One of the drawers of the desk comes out by itself in a kind of organic protractile movement . . .'

Nabokov the scenarist is no more fettered by precedents and probability than Nabokov the novelist. Let there be Felliniesque equivalents to his book's rapturous prose, as when Humbert's mother dies and 'her graceful specter floats up above the black cliffs holding a parasol and blowing kisses to her husband and child who stand below, looking up, hand in hand.' Humbert reads Charlotte's declaration of love and 'In one SHOT, he is dressed as a gowned professor in another as a routine Hamlet, in a third, as a dilapidated Poe.' The screenplay provides charts, maps, freeze frames – movie devices that in 1961 were still fresh, indeed impudent, ways of telling a story. It offers adverbial clues to performers in cameo roles: 'Dog (*perfunctorily*): Woof.' And in the scene of Lo's seduction of Hum, the screenwriter murmurs tentative advice to the director: 'With a burst of rough glee, she puts her mouth to his ear (could one reproduce this hot moist sound, the tickle and the buzz, the vibration, the thunder of her whisper?).'

The odd thing is that Kubrick streamlined Nabokov's script into a well-made story. The novelist wrote a buoyantly cinematic movie, which could exist only on the page.

Line 67: When Kubrick put my darling on the screen

She was a breach baby: she arrived foot first. Fade in to a cluster of satiny drapes resting on a flat surface. The opening credits are fanfared by the swelling arpeggios of Nelson Riddle's theme music. The words 'James B. Harris and Stanley Kubrick's' disappear from the screen, and just before the word 'Lolita' appears a girl's left foot drops into the frame, from top right. From the left of the screen a man's left hand cradles the foot and applies nail polish to each nail, occasionally placing cotton wads between the toes. The credits continue to fade in and out on her ankle, like wash-off tattoos. At no time does the foot touch the bed; in a cramp-defying aerial act, it rests in the man's hand. The toes are dutiful, disciplined, rising only when the cotton is applied; only once do they wriggle, just to let you know there is life in them.

This is the movie metonymy of a sort familiar in Saul Bass credit sequences of the 50s and 60s (the jagged arm for *The Man With the Golden Arm*, the undulating cat for a prostitute in *A Walk on the Wild*

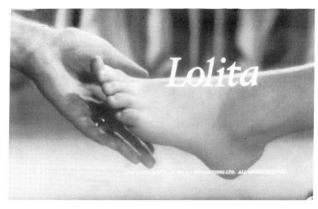

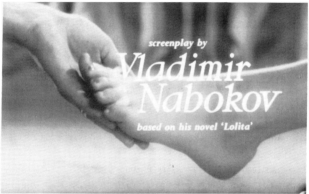

The opening titles

Side). These clever titles, by the British firm Chambers & Partners, posit a seesaw equilibrium between man and child, or father and daughter, or Jack and Jill, or john and call girl – he is the slave, painting her toes; she is the slave, acceding to his whim – that the rest of the film (especially the scene in which Mason paints Lo's toenails) gives the lie to. Or perhaps this is a fantasy of Humbert's, a modest dream of paradise, where a nymphet will agree to dwell for ever in the double-bolted penthouse of his devotion.

Oswald Morris, who had photographed four John Huston films and two for Tony Richardson, was no fan of Kubrick's. In 1990 he named Kubrick as one of two directors he would never work with again. On *Lolita*, Morris recalled, 'He'd say, "Now I want this scene lit as though there's just one light bulb in the middle of the set." ... Fifteen minutes later he'd come back and say, "What are all those lights? I told you just one light-bulb." I said, "It's basically and faithfully lit as if with one light-bulb." ... I defied him, you see. ... So we used to fight. ... It all got a bit boring, inquest after inquest about the lighting.'

Lolita may have been dark by Morris's standards – cheekbones don't glisten, exactly, in the old William Daniels style at MGM – but the movie looked creamy compared to earlier Kubricks. The jagged

chiaroscuro of *Killer's Kiss* and *The Killing* are softened to flatter the actors (Mason, so distinguished; Lyon, so succulent) at the expense of the characters (Humbert, less leprous; Lolita, less manipulative). Only Quilty, as Dr Zempf, gets the single-bulb treatment. He sits in the darkened living room opposite Humbert. A thin light falls on the end table between them, on which stands an empty Coke bottle with a straw in it, an objective correlative for Lolita and her connivance in Quilty's game. (The advertising logo for the film was a flower vase with a straw in it.) In most other scenes the lighting is traditional, comforting. It tells the audience: this is not a melodrama, where nasty people do naughty things that should be seen only in garish neon through venetian blinds; this is a drama, where nice people have sad problems.

The film's tempo may also have been destined to reassure the viewer. In the late 50s and early 60s movies were longer than ever. A film of *Lolita*'s running time, 152 minutes, may have been unusual ten years before; but Hollywood was starting to dodder in the twilight time of the studio system. Directors asserted their authority by slowing the pace and accenting the mood; screenwriters built scenes more meticulously, elaborately; actors who had been schooled in the Method found eloquence in inarticulateness, with its stumbling and pauses.

Lolita with a Coke

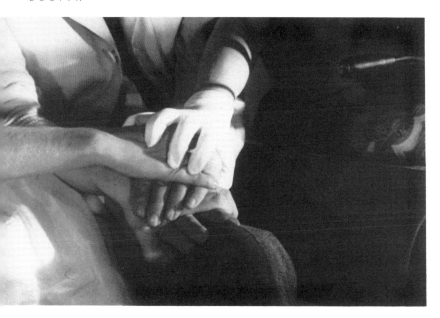

Above: 'The pyramid of affection'

Below: 'Unaware that Charlotte is about to snap his picture'

Lolita was a commuter on this scenic railway to senescence.

Kubrick manages some funny, telling vignettes: mood-grabbers in expert cinematic shorthand. The famous drive-in scene – where Humbert, sitting between Lolita and Charlotte at a showing of Hammer Films' *The Curse of Frankenstein*, feels their trembling hands upon his own, disengages one hand from Charlotte to attend to Lo, then realises that Charlotte's hand has joined the pyramid of affection – takes but forty seconds. Another scene is twenty-two seconds: Humbert in the garden, peeking at Lolita's hula-hoop exertions, unaware that Charlotte is about to snap his picture. These are pure movie moments.

Most of *Lolita*'s story, though, is spun out in play-length sequences of very few shots, the camera moving to make room for the actors but mostly staying near the transparent fourth wall. Each scene has its own dramatic arc, described at leisure. These set pieces may run for seven minutes (cha cha cha), eight minutes (the summer dance), ten (the killing of Quilty), seventeen (the morning of Charlotte's death). However much Harris and Kubrick cut down Nabokov's screenplay, they still left scenes with plenty of meat, and some fat.

Line 68 (a): words made whispers

In a Lubitsch comedy the lovers would close a bedroom door and leave the doings inside to the viewer's imagination. In this Kubrick comedy people whisper, literally, when they're not screaming at each other. Charlotte whispers a reminder to Quilty about their afternoon affair. 'Did I do that?' he asks wolfishly. 'Did I? Well!' Quilty, in the company of Vivian Darkbloom, is constantly making suggestive eye contact, talking voiceless words. And in the one conversation (at a gas station) between the film's chronic heartbreakers, Lo talks to Quilty so cautiously that we don't hear her and don't see him.

Pretty obviously, Kubrick feared that if the characters were to give voice to what they were thinking, everybody would land in jail. That's why the double entendres slide by without being capped by a rejoinder: if the characters in the movie don't get the jokes, maybe the censor won't either. When Quilty asks Humbert if he can keep serving at table tennis because 'I sorta like to have it up *this* end, you know', Hum does not so much as flinch at Quilty's allusion to sodomy. Nor does Lolita move a muscle (though Charlotte's head does a half-swivel) when Humbert tells her, apropos the dinner Lady Haze cooked before vamping him that 'Your mother created a magnificent spread!'

Such were the contortions deemed mandatory to get a film in 1962. Today it all appears childish. But the strategy also indicates that sex is a kid's game, like whispering down the lane: all innuendo, excited giggling, raised eyebrows, and getting things wrong.

That's certainly the message of Lolita's bedroom scene in the Enchanted Hunters. Having twice chased Humbert out of her bed the night before, Lo wakes up and discovers Hum on a collapsible cot, collapsed on the floor. Throughout, she is above him, looking down at his befuddled face, his quivering anticipation. She's in charge, deciding whether and when. Her voice is, for once, intimate and inflected. She tells him she wants to play a game: 'I learned some real good games in camp. One in particular was fun. ... I played it with Charlie. ... You sure you can't guess what game I'm talking about?' Hum, playing dumb, says, 'I'm not a very good guesser', and Lo whispers in his ear. 'I don't know what game you played,' he insists, and again she whispers. She is an ace at all these games – some learned at camp, others in her blood. She stares meaningfully at Humbert, giggles at his wan jokes, compares tans, strokes his stubbly face, toys with his hair. And finally,

in a close-up of her guileless smile that fills the screen, she says, 'All righty then', and Daddy's Little Girl, the angel-whore, comes down to his level to show him how it's done.

Her whisper says it all. Speak Lo when you speak love.

Line 68 (b): twelve made teen

'I've put off reading *Lolita* for six years,' Groucho Marx announced when the novel appeared. 'Until she's eighteen.'

By casting Sue Lyon, Kubrick met Groucho halfway: she was fourteen when got the part, fifteen when she completed the film. But chronology has little to do with movie iconography. Lyon looked a trim seventeen; she was a nymphet emeritus. The gap between the ages of Nabokov's Lolita (twelve-and-a-half) and Kubrick's (say, fourteen-and-a-half) also marks a crucial change from novel to film. The book is about child abuse; the movie is about the wiles a teenage girl might have learned in those two years: an awareness of her power over men.

Lyon's first appearance in the movie – she reclines on a blanket in the Haze garden, wearing a flowered bikini, a huge feathered straw hat, the eyewear that came to be known as 'Lolita sunglasses', and on her mouth a blank expression that appraises Humbert and allows him to appraise her – all this said sex. It also told the audience, at a glance, that the film of *Lolita* was not the book. Not that the mass movie audience had read the book; they may have known only that it was about a man who liked little girls. But here was a big girl. Lyon in that garden was not a 'potential' anything; she was already there. Her unforced insolence announced that she could take care of herself. She had the poise of a girl aware of her body and its beguilements. She might be handled, but not moulded. There is nothing a nympholept could teach her. She is already taut.

She watches Hum with smirky satisfaction, not because she is attracted to him but because she is amused by the effect she has on him. In an early scene one Saturday in the lodger's study, she lightly ironises his secrecy in locking his incriminating diary in a desk drawer ('Fraid somebody's gonna steal your ideas and sell 'em to Hollywood?') before allowing him to flirt with her. Poor scholar! Hum's notion of a first date is to read her a poem, 'Annabel Lee', by 'the divine Edgar'. To Lo this is like school at weekends. She has a cuter idea. 'Put your head back,' she

Lyon's first appearance

commands, picking up an untouched fried egg on his breakfast dish. 'Put your head back! Open your mouth. You can have *one* little bite.' Miserable, delirious Humbert obeys. A *chomp!* for the chump. And a coup for Lyon; she is as much in control of the scene as Lo.

Harris and Kubrick had good reasons to make a Lola out of Lolita. Here are a few. The film would then be released. Humbert's love for her would be an obsession but not a perversion. The audience could share his appreciation for her. A slightly older girl was likely to be a more secure actress. Harris and Kubrick wanted to sign the girl to a multipicture contract (they did sign Lyon), and an evident teenager would be suitable for a wider variety of roles. Also, the same actress must play Lo at the cusp of teenagery and, in her last scene, at seventeen. Lyon could do that; she is already the superior counterfeit of young womanhood. But any girl who could pass for the later Lolita could not be convincing as the true Lolita.

Line 69 (a): Back roads made backlots

Lolita is a road map of American culture in the postwar decade, whose signifiers are explained by Appel, genial cartographer, in *Nabokov's Dark*

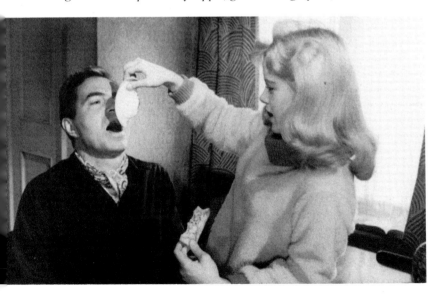

Cinema. It is also a road movie in embryo; it is as curious about motel architecture and diner menus as it is about the mismatched man and girl who have sex in those beds and get sick on that food. It measures lives by inches (Lolita, four feet ten in one sock) and miles (on the odometer of Humbert's Melmoth). Most of the book is set in 1947, the year of *Out of the Past*, the year after *Detour*, the year before *They Live by Night*, two years before *Gun Crazy*. Moviegoers, if not readers, were used to the picture of two people, in the front seat of a car, staring ahead, nothing to say, anticipating a crash.

The young Kubrick had made his name with location shooting: in the San Gabriel Mountains for *Fear and Desire*, in Times Square for *Killer's Kiss*, in Germany for *Paths of Glory*. But with *Spartacus* he had realised that only in a studio could he and the actors concentrate on, and thus control, their craft. 'Whereas outside everything fades away,' he wrote in 1960, 'inside there is a kind of inner focusing of psychical energy.' Besides, American cinema was largely stagebound; it might globetrot to Paris or Thailand for exotic vistas, but it wouldn't go out on Route 66 for the local colour. Leave that to Robert Frank in the late 50s; wait for *Easy Rider* in the late 60s.

Do decades have personalities? Do tectonic shifts in mores occur at convenient ten-year intervals? Not exactly, but if an American had fallen asleep in the summer of 1947 (when Nabokov's novel is set) and awoken ten years after (when Kubrick's film is set), he or she would have noticed and heard a difference. In 1947 the sun was unclouded, the nights were *noir*ish, and kids were, on the whole, still kids. For that time, Lolita's precocity was nearly as extreme as Humbert's lust. But in the Age of Rock, Lo might be just another avid teen, one more rebel without a clue. And Humbert would be an almost typically square parent or lecherous suburbanite, a Daddy Long Leg.

Line 69 (b): US made UK

Nabokov, a Russian, came to America, stayed there for more than twenty years, learned its ways and highways, and wrote a novel that (according to Boyd) traverses every one of the contiguous United States. To make a film of that novel, Kubrick, an American whose two previous films had been set in Europe, left the United States for Britain, and has stayed there ever since.

The local fauna that Nabokov so meticulously studied and reshaped made *Lolita*'s landscape unique, and made Humbert's disease – madness, complicated by genius – rare indeed. Kubrick, having ameliorated Humbert's ailment into a more general, genteel neurosis, needed a generic look for the exteriors, and shooting in Britain gave him that, by default (though, Morris says, 'he did have a second unit over there, who brought back miles of stuff for the driving scenes'). Hum and Lo were now speeding down Anyroad, USA, or UK, and if the viewer inferred from this that they were Anyfolks, all the better. With disruptive car horns and quirky passers-by removed, 'A Motel Room at the Kozy Kabins Lodge' became 'motel room', as blandly furnished and exquisitely metaphorical as Sartre's Hell in *No Exit*.

Kubrick's *Lolita* was in essence a chamber play, a story of four people playing sick games inside one another's skulls. And in the absence of the novel's erotic pyrotechnics, the four actors needed the cocoon of a sound stage to marshal the reserves of comic subtlety needed for their work. So their *Lolita* suffers less from the loss of locus than Nabokov's (the screenplay version) would have.

The Eady pact specified that 80 per cent of the film's labour costs during production would go to British workers, and that all but two of

'Mind if I dance with your girl, Humbert?'

the featured actors (Winters and Lyon) must be British subjects. Some of the others were English, some Canadian; some could counterfeit American dialogue more persuasively than others. The best ones fell into that bland insidiousness familiar to anyone who has listened to Kubrick films – to the chipper cynicism of Adolphe Menjou in *Paths of Glory*, the seductiveness of Olivier in *Spartacus*, the computer-knows-best musicality of HAL 9000 (Douglas Rain) in *2001*. This sonorous voice held a warning: I'm normal. Don't trust me.

Kubrick's most subversive suburbanites are Charlotte's best friends, John Farlow (Jerry Stovin), a lawyer, and his wife Jean (Diana Decker). With their bland mid-American looks Decker is an even more proper Donna Reed, Stovin could be one of the Four Glads. They have only two scenes – at the summer dance and, briefly, in Humbert's bathroom after Charlotte's death – but in their few minutes of screen time they create a satyrical style so deft they seem hardly aware of it. They have a festive depravity; in their banter, an invitation to group sex sounds like a church raffle ticket. 'Mind if I dance with your girl, Humbert?' John asks with bizarre bonhomie. 'We could, uh, sorta swap partners.' Then Jean takes Humbert aside and, when he deflects her suggestion that he is making Charlotte 'glow', she says, sweet as a sugar cube laced with LSD, 'When you get to know me you'll find I'm extremely broad-minded. In fact, John and I, we're *both* broad-minded.'

This is as blatant as Hollywood sex chat could be in the *Pillow Talk* days. Kubrick knew it; so did Humbert. At dinner à *deux*, Haze prepares Hum for the news that she is sending Lolita to Camp Climax by saying, 'I have a glorious surprise for us.' Humbert muses: 'The Farlows have been arrested?' No, but if cinema's blue noses had paid closer attention to these two foreigners masquerading as American wife-swappers, Kubrick might have been called in for questioning.

Line 70: green made gold

Lolita was green no more; the child had ripened into Betty Co–ed. And *Lolita* was no longer *2 Men and a Baby*; it was *Teen-age Rebel*. That Edmund Goulding film of 1956, and most of the era's teen dramas (*Rebel Without a Cause* being a notable exception), were how-to-cope manuals for fretful moms and dads. In the 90s most Hollywood movies are about precocious kids trying to teach adults how to be human. If

Adrian Lyne ever makes his *Lolita*, you can bet it will be the story of an abused child. And why not? After all, the novel was.

Kubrick's *Lolita* is the story of an abused stepfather. Humbert is the modern American parent, which is to say, the scold and the slave – which is to say, Charlotte. Both Hum and Haze see Lo's budding sexuality as a threat to their own predatory vigour. And when they can't be parents, they try to be kids: Charlotte as the teen vamp, Hum as Lo's possessive pal. In the scene where Hum paints Lo's toenails he is stung when his mistress moans about not having any fun. 'You have all the fun in the world,' exclaims this dutiful dad. 'We have fun together, don't we? Whenever you want something, I buy it for you automatically. I take you to concerts, to museums, to movies. I do all the housework ...' It is the voice of the insufficiently loved, with the lover-loser's festering suspicions and quicksand gullibility. And the saddest part is that Humbert doesn't even hear Charlotte's voice screaming through his carefully modulated tones. We become whom we hate.

As for the gold: *Lolita* was a decent-size hit in its 1962 release. Its returns were meagre compared to those of the year's expensive epics: *How the West Was Won* earned MGM nearly $21 million at the North American box office, *Lawrence of Arabia* $19 million for Columbia, *The Longest Day* $17,600,000 for 20th Century-Fox. Still, *Lolita*'s domestic release returned $3,700,000 to MGM, more than double the cost of production. Harris and Kubrick made a tidy profit, thanks to a deal they cut with Seven Arts. As owners of Sue Lyon's contract, they got a percentage of the salary she received for appearing in Huston's *The Night of the Iguana* and Ford's *Seven Women*. The partners broke up during pre-production of *Dr Strangelove*: Kubrick wanted to produce his own films (as he has done ever since) and Harris wanted to direct (as he has done from *The Bedford Incident* in 1965 to *Boiling Point* in 1993).

Mason remained an international star of the second magnitude and an actor of the first magnetism. Sellers became Inspector Clouzot and learned to mangle French as amusingly as he did American English. Winters gleaned an Oscar nomination for overacting underwater in *The Poseidon Adventure*. Lyon, in an interview in the 70s, after her career had gone south and her youth had gone sour, declared that *Lolita* had warped her life.

Line 77: Fitzgerald

F. Scott Fitzgerald (1896–1940), failed screenwriter. His only screenplay credit in three tours of Hollywood was *Three Comrades* (1938). Producer Joseph L. Mankiewicz rewrote Fitzgerald's script.

Line 80: shade

John Shade wrote the poem *Pale Fire*, a suburban epic in 999 lines of iambic pentameter, whose thousandth line ('I was the shadow of the waxwing slain') is its first. I.e., the poem doubles back on itself, the way the screenplay and film of *Lolita* do, or Humbert and Quilty, or the numbers on the Melmoth odometer in the book and movie – the 09999.9 rolling its eyes upwards into 10000.0. Charles Kinbote, a neighbour of Shade's, wrote a commentary on the poem. Both works (Shade's verse and Kinbote's converse) were published by Nabokov in 1962.

Line 85: the true *Lolita*

My official imaginary movie version of *Lolita* was made, in 1959, by a troika of Kubrick, Vincente Minnelli and Douglas Sirk. It starred Mason, Lyon (two crucial years younger), Patricia Neal as Charlotte and Lenny Bruce as Quilty. It was told in flashback by Humbert, speaking to his prison psychiatrist John Ray, Jr (who might also have been played by Bruce). It insinuated, for detection by the careful viewer, that Humbert was not always honest with Ray or himself. It allowed Lolita to suggest, to this same watcher, that she was in Quilty's thrall. It displayed Humbert's sentimental sadism, the better to uncover Quilty's masterful evil. It was faithful to the book. It broke your heart.

Here are a few telling scenes, all from the novel:

On a family outing at Our Glass Lake, Lolita finds a speck in her eye. Hum offers to lick it out. Lo obliges.

A few hours before they become lovers, sleepy Lo wakes, drinks a glass of water, 'and then, with an infantile gesture that carried more charm than any carnal caress, wiped her lips against my shoulder.'

Humbert is ecstatic at the girl's need for him, even as a poor substitute for Kleenex.

A littered landscape of Esso stations and ptomaine diners, Patti and Eddie on the juke box, Kozy Kabins stocked with gift-wrapped soap in the bathroom and a child bride shivering in bed.

In a motel room, sleepy As Lo stirs. Humbert, her doting maid, brings a cup of coffee to the bedside. As Lo reflexively reaches for it, Hum, her insatiable master, wags a stern finger. Just as reflexively, she kisses his naked chest.

Lolita, pinioned in bed, trying to claw her father-lover's back with her nails. Can't; she's bitten them to the nub.

Humbert cries while making love ('It may interest physiologists to learn that I have the ability to shed torrents of tears through the other tempest'). Lolita, little girl lost, but not to Humbert, cries only to herself ('her sobs in the night – every night, every night – once I feigned sleep').

Trooper Quilty shadows the Melmoth from a discreet, worrying distance. Hum is pained, properly paranoid. 'And all the while I was aware of a private blaze on my right: her joyful eye, her flaming cheek.' A movie might not capture the literary double duty of 'flaming cheek' (flushed excitement, reckless arrogance), but it could suggest, by the fire animating Lo's features, that she is thrilled by the pursuit.

On a tennis court at the last motel stop for Humbert and Lolita, the girl throws a wet little red ball to a dog, and 'there was an ecstasy, a madness about her frolics that was too much of a glad thing'. Lo is performing this scene for her favourite director, her observant lover, her number-one fan – Quilty. Humbert looks at this porcine drooler and sees his evil twin, then realises that Quilty is, no, his *perfect* twin: Humbert rampant.

For once, in the voice-over, cut to Humbert's face in prison as he admits, or insists, 'You see, I loved her. It was love at first sight, at last sight, at ever and ever sight.'

When Humbert comes to visit pregnant Dolly, she smokes a cigarette. Her gestures exactly mimic Charlotte's.

And she might show some sympathy to the gargoyle whose paint has chipped to reveal the wan, broken old man sitting on her couch.

The final scene is still in the lab.

Line 88: nut with net

Nabokov was a distinguished lepidopterist. He discovered and named a number of butterflies, and a few were named after him.

In one of the many scenes from the *Lolita* screenplay that was scrapped before filming, Nabokov surfaces as himself – 'that nut with the net', as Dolores Haze describes him – and pedantically corrects Humbert's ignorance of lepidoptery before confessing that he hasn't the vaguest idea where he is.

I hereby wish him to be in Telluride, Colorado, which is just up the road from the little town of Dolores.

Line 90: tel lurid e

In the winter, Telluride (elevation: 8,746 feet) is a popular ski resort. In late summer, the town is host to North America's most intimate and intense film festival. In July 1951, though, it was a summer home for Nabokov; he and his wife Véra were there on a lepidoptery expedition. The town is significant in a few ways: 'It was at such of our head-quarters as Telluride, Colorado ... that *Lolita* was energetically resumed in the evenings or on cloudy days,' he relates in the Afterword to the book, and it was there he 'caught the first known female of *Lycaeides sublivens* Nabokov'. Telluride, as the author noted in a letter to Edmund Wilson, was 'an old-fashioned, absolutely touristless mining town full of the most helpful, charming people ... and when you hike from there [up the craggy slopes] ... all you hear are the voices of children playing in the streets – delightful!'

With this sound, Nabokov ended his novel in 'a last mirage of wonder and hopelessness'. One day after his step-daughter's disappearance, Humbert pulls over to the side of a mountain road. 'I grew aware of a melodious unity of sounds rising like vapour from a small mining town that lay at my feet... What I heard was but the melody of children at play, nothing but that, and so limpid was the air that within this vapour of blended voices, majestic and minute, remote and magically near, frank and divinely enigmatic – one could hear now and then, as if released, an almost articulate spurt of vivid laughter, or the crack of a bat, or the clatter of a toy wagon... and then I knew that the hopelessly poignant thing was not Lolita's absence from my side, but the absence of her voice from that concord.'

In this beautiful reverie of revelation and flagellation, Humbert accuses himself of a crime worse than raping a child; he has killed her childhood. As such, *Lolita* is sociologically far-sighted: it predicts the United States of the 1990s, for whose precocious children sex is not a diet, or even a banquet, but an All You Can Eat fast-food spread. The price tag is an adolescence that crash-lands in premature middle age. Nabokov saw this fast-spin cycle of ecstasy and desperation in the elfin, orphaned figure of Dolores Haze: born 1935, sex adept at twelve, concubine at thirteen, house guest of a bizarre cult at fourteen, then waitress and wife, then expectant mother, then . . . ' "Mrs. Richard F. Schiller" died in childbed, giving birth to a stillborn girl, on Christmas Day 1952, in Gray Star, a settlement in the remotest Northwest.'

In the remotest northwest corner of California, there is a town called Loleta in the county of Humboldt.

Final scene from the imaginary movie of *Lolita*:

Humbert on the mountain road. The unearthly music. The mist evaporates and, through a series of encroaching dissolves, we see town, school, schoolyard. A dozen kids, giddy, unshadowed by care, with nothing finer to do than play tag. Our eyes relax into this idyll for a moment. Then the ghost of Lolita as Humbert never allowed her to be – not childlike or childish: a child – slowly materialises and shares in the lazy fun. She looks up at the camera. Reaction shot of Humbert. She looks down and disappears into the haze of his undying pain.

Line 94: flits away, as in a dream

Lolita, from book to film, was a wet dream that got dry-cleaned into a daydream. The novel was about lust that ascended into love; the movie is about love, unrequited and unrepentant. Harris says he and Kubrick really believed Trilling's comment that *Lolita* is not about sex but about love. In their version, love is everywhere. It even peeks into the first and last rooms that Humbert and Lolita share: at the Enchanted Hunters, where man and girl can stay because 'Captain Love', a police officer, has cancelled his reservation; and at the hospital where Hum, kissing Lo goodbye, is eyed suspiciously by 'Nurse Love', who presumably helps Quilty spirit Lo out of Humbert's arms.

Humbert has finished his 'We have fun, don't we?' plaint (*see note to line 70*). Lo gives the Look That Melts and says, 'Come here.' But she's not offering him sex; she's affording him the honour of telling her he loves her – 'completely'. We know that already; it's been in Mason's eyes and voice. His crush on Lyon's Lolita is effulgently evident; her betrayal of him is artfully hidden (she's only indulging his ardour so that he will give her permission to appear in Quilty's play).

'Naturally I regret that the film could not be more erotic,' said Kubrick, to Alexander Walker. 'The eroticism of the story served a very important purpose in the book: it obscured any hint that Humbert loved Lolita. ... It was very important to delay an awareness of his love until the end of the story. I'm afraid that this was all too obvious in the film. But in my view this is the only justifiable criticism.' It's a significant criticism, though. Moviegoers are denied the therapeutic revelation that a monster can be sanctified. They can infer only that Lolita was a coarse, naive witch – her mother, but smarter and crueller – and that Humbert was a fool for getting in her way. Further, since they know that Humbert has already killed Quilty, there is no suspense in the final scene, the return to the evil man's lair. Unless . . . Let's look again.

Final scene from the Kubrick version of *Lolita*:

The 137-minute flashback is over, and Humbert finds himself repeating Scene One. The same foggy road tags along after his white car; we think of other dates with *déjà vu* destiny in *The Shining* and *Dead of Night*. Humbert enters Castle Quilty, wandering through the same cluttered dreamscape. Once more he walks through the living room and calls out, 'Quilty. Quilty!' And again we see the easy chair, draped in a sheet, from which the playwright will emerge. All is as before, floating in our eyes with the familiarity of a recurring dream.

Except that, this time, something is missing: the liquor bottle that had teetered on Quilty's head and, with its crashing, announced his presence. The villain, it seems, has vanished. And Humbert has walked into a parallel nightmare, where his righteous revenge may never be satisfied.

Line 95: freedom in a cage

In 1962 any film of *Lolita* was obliged to be circumspect, slyly euphemistic, grounded in metaphor: Professor Humbert on his best behaviour. The movie needed to be almost as opaque a reflection of this enormous, mysterious, heartbreaking novel as Quilty's airy drama *The Lady Who Loved Lightning* was of the playwright's subversive agenda for the children who appeared in it.

Kubrick seemingly had the choice of making *Lolita* the censors' way, or not making it at all. He did something more devious: he made it their way *his way*. This time he was no Spartacus, come to split the shackles of the commercial cinema. He was one of those wily Roman senators, Crassus or Gracchus or even Caesar, plotting to seize as much as was within his power, as gracefully as was within his craft – to find, in this cage of commerce and accommodation, a kind of freedom. As much freedom, at least, as the Hollywood codes would allow.

'I found myself maturing,' Humbert writes, 'in a civilisation which allows a man of twenty-five to court a girl of sixteen but not a girl of twelve.' Timing is all, in life and art. If Humbert could have waited just a few more years, from twelve to sixteen, he might have courted Lolita and won, if not her heart, at least society's official sanction. But then, at sixteen Dolores Haze would not have been Lolita. If Kubrick could have waited just a few years – for commercial film to grow up, to get down and dirty, and for his natural boldness to assert itself – he surely would have made a *Lolita* true to his ambitions and the novel's elusive heart. But he and Lolita met at the wrong time. He was too young; she, in his eyes, too old.

The *Lolita* Kubrick did make is a very good film, a vivacious variant on a treacherous theme, with every subtlety and subversion a commercial movie artist could bring to it. It is also very much a film of its time: glamorous and measured; an 'adult' picture about kids, seen from an adult's perspective; precisely performed and beautifully attentive to the actors; timid and defiant in surprising ways; cosseted by convention, yet looking chic in its straitjacket.

Nabokov's *Lolita* is a great novel, transcending the critical fashions of its time or ours. Then it sounded like a sadist's sob, later like the Olympian laugh of a social satirist. Now, under those harsh melodies, we can detect the music of children at play, in a field sown with landmines. The kids are all bright with promise and threat, all doomed to shuck their innocence too quickly, as Lolita did the nymphetry that Humbert imposed on her. In their perishability, this concord is as precious as a memory or fantasy of our collective youth. An awful, tender world explodes from the friction of Nabokov's words. In the reader's mind this world forms images and evokes emotions as indelible as any committed to film.

Line 99: Who was that monarch?

'I have a fair inkling of my literary afterlife,' Nabokov wrote in 1963. 'I have felt the breeze of certain promises. No doubt there will be ups and downs, long periods of slump. With the Devil's connivance, I open a newspaper of 2063 and in some article on the books page I find: "Nobody reads Nabokov or Fulmerford today." Awful question: who is this unfortunate Fulmerford?'

Perhaps, in 2063, nobody will read. Movies, or their technological descendants, will be the only literature. And Nabokov's novels will be footnotes in the filmographies of Kubrick, Richardson, Skolimowski, Fassbinder. But, anyway, let me hope: for a living, faithful rendering of Nabokov's *Lolita* screenplay; for a free and secure Russian cinema to bring *The Gift* and *Invitation to a Beheading* to the screen; for film-makers to bring to their work the bravado and tact that Nabokov scrupulously lavished in his novels. I would also hope for the publication of his final, nearly completed work, which Nabokov's son Dmitri (according to Field) 'enthusiastically claimed bid fair to be better than any of his previous novels.' Its very title – *The Original of Laura* – stirs a Nabokolept's fancy. What pleasures might reside there: nymphets and cinema, Petrarch and Preminger. I anticipate enchantments.

In another futuristic nightmare, all films will have been nuked and only books remain. Then a reader might find this volume and wonder, 'Who is this unfortunate Kubrick?' He is a fellow unlucky enough to have met Dolores Haze when she was a teenager and not a nymphet, so she declined to share her immortality with him. But the director learned from *Lolita* and willed his own fortune. He became Stanley Kubrick.

Imagine these two men on the road, as Humbert and Lolita so often were, following signs that direct them to their artistic fates. For Nabokov, *Lolita* was a destination, an apotheosis of the themes that occupied him all his life. For Kubrick, it was a signpost to the land he would soon inhabit and conquer.

CREDITS

· ·

GB
1961
Production company
© A.A Productions Ltd.
An Anya Production S.A. –
Transworld Pictures S.A.
Production
A Metro-Goldwyn-Mayer
Presentation in association
with Seven Arts Productions
A James B. Harris & Stanley
Kubrick Film
GB trade show
4 September 1962
GB release
September 1962
GB distributor
Metro Goldwyn Mayer
Pictures
US copyright
31 December 1961
US release
13 June 1962
US distributor
Metro-Goldwyn-Mayer Inc.

Producer
James B. Harris
Production supervisor
Raymond Anzarut
Production manager
Robert Sterne
Production secretary
Joan Purcell
Producer's secretary
Josephine Baker
Production accountant
Jack Smith
Assistant accountant
Doreen Wood
Secretaries
Jack Smith, Jennifer Halford
Director
Stanley Kubrick
2nd unit director
Dennis Stock
Assistant director
René Dupont
2nd assistant director
Roy Millichip
3rd assistant director
John Danischewsky
Director's secretary
Stella Magee
Screenplay
Vladimir Nabokov from his
own novel
Special writer
David Sylvester
Continuity
Pamela Davies
Assistant continuity
Joyce Herlihy
Photography (b & w)
Oswald Morris
Camera operator
Denys Coop
Focus puller
Jimmy Turrell
Clapper loader
Michael Rutter
Camera grip
A. Osborne

Electrics gaffer
W. Thompson
**Music composed and
conducted**
Nelson Riddle
Orchestration
Gil Grau
'Lolita' theme
Bob Harris
Editor
Anthony Harvey
Assistant editor
Lois Gray
2nd assistant editor
W. W. Armour
Art director
Bill Andrews
Associate art director
Sidney Cain
Chief draughtsman
Frank Wilson
Draughtsmen
John Siddall, Roy Dorman
Scenic artist
A. Van Montagu
Set decorator
Andrew Low
Set dresser
Peter James
Construction manager
Harry Phipps
Miss Winters' costumes
Gene Coffin
Wardrobe supervisor
Elsa Fennell
Wardrobe mistress
Barbara Gillett
Wardrobe assistant
Wyn Keeley
Make-up
George Partleton
Assistant make-up
Stella Morris
Hairdresser
Betty Glasow
Casting director
James Liggat

Titles
Chambers & Partners
Production buyer
Terry Parr
Unit publicist
Enid Jones
Publicity secretary
Amy Allen
Stills
Joe Pearce
Dubbing editor
Winston Ryder
Sound recorders
Len Shilton, H. L. Bird
Boom operator
Dan Wortham
Assistant boom operators
Peter Carnody, T. Staples
Sound maintenance
L. Grimmel, Jack Lovelace
153 minutes
13,798 feet

James Mason
Humbert Humbert
Shelley Winters
Charlotte Haze
Sue Lyon
Lolita Haze
Peter Sellers
Clare Quilty
Gary Cockrell
Richard 'Dick' Schiller, Lolita's husband
Jerry Stovin
John Farlow
Diana Decker
Jean Farlow
Lois Maxwell
Nurse Mary Love
Cec Linder
Physician
Bill Greene
George Swine
Shirley Douglas
Mrs Starch
Marianne Stone
Vivian Darkbloom
Marion Mathie
Miss Lebone
James Dyrenforth
Beale
Maxine Holden
Hospital receptionist
John Harrison
Tom
Colin Maitland
Charlie
C. Denier Warren
Potts
Roland Brand
Bill
Terence Kilburn
and *(uncredited)*
Suzanne Gibbs
Mona Farlow
Isobel Lucas
Louise, the Haze maid
Roberta Shore
Lorna

Eric Lane
Roy
Irvin Allen
Andre, hospital attendant
Craig Sams
Rex

Credits checked by Markku Salmi. The print of *Lolita* in the National Film and Television Archive was specially acquired from MGM/UA.

DIBLIOGRAPHY

· ·

Agel, Jerome, *The Making of Kubrick's 2001* (New York: New American Library, 1970).

Appel, Alfred, Jr., *Nabokov's Dark Cinema* (New York: Oxford University Press, 1974).

Appel, Alfred, Jr. (ed.), *The Annotated Lolita* (New York: Vintage Books, 1991).

Boyd, Brian, *Vladimir Nabokov: The Russian Years* (Princeton: Princeton University Press, 1990).

Boyd, Brian, *Vladimir Nabokov: The American Years* (Princeton: Princeton University Press, 1992).

de Grazia, Edward, *Girls Lean Back Everywhere: The Law of Obscenity and the Assault on Genius* (New York: Random House, 1992).

Field, Andrew, *Nabokov: His Life in Art* (London: Hodder & Stoughton, 1967).

Field, Andrew, *VN: The Life and Art of Vladimir Nabokov* (New York: Crown, 1986).

Gelmis, Joseph (ed.), *The Film Director as Superstar* (Garden City, New York: Doubleday, 1970).

Greene, Graham, *The Pleasure Dome: Film Criticism, 1935–40* (London: Secker & Warburg, 1972).

Kagan, Norman, *The Cinema of Stanley Kubrick* (New York: Continuum, 1989).

Katz, Ephraim, *The Film Encyclopedia* (New York: Harper & Row, 1979).

Mason, James, *Before I Forget* (London: Hamish Hamilton, 1981).

Nabokov, Vladimir, *Laughter in the Dark* (Indianapolis: Bobbs Merrill, 1938).

Nabokov, Vladimir, *Despair* (New York: Putnam,1965).

Nabokov, Vladimir, *The Enchanter* (New York: Putnam, 1986).

Nabokov, Vladimir, *Lolita* (New York: Fawcett, 1959).

Nabokov, Vladimir, *King, Queen, Knave* (New York: McGraw Hill, 1968).

Nabokov, Vladimir, *Pale Fire* (New York: Putnam, 1962).

Nabokov, Vladimir, *Lolita: A Screenplay* (New York: McGraw Hill, 1974).

Nabokov, Vladimir, *Strong Opinions* (New York: McGraw Hill, 1975).

Nelson, Thomas Allen, *Kubrick: Inside a Film Artist's Maze* (Bloomington: Indiana University Press, 1982).

Sarris, Andrew (ed.), *Interviews with Film Directors* (Indianapolis: Bobbs Merrill, 1968).

Walker, Alexander, *The Celluloid Sacrifice* (London: Michael Joseph, 1966).

Winters, Shelley, *Shelley II* (New York: William Morrow, 1984).

ALSO PUBLISHED

**If you would like further information
about future BFI Film Classics or
about other books on film, media and
popular culture from BFI Publishing,
please write to:**

**BFI Film Classics
British Film Institute
21 Stephen Street
London
W1P 1PL**